the Greatest
of These

Biblical Moorings of Love

JOHN
INDERMARK

Abingdon Press
Nashville

THE GREATEST OF THESE
BIBLICAL MOORINGS OF LOVE

Copyright © 2011 by Abingdon Press

This book is printed on acid-free paper.

Library of Congress Cataloging-in-Publication Data

Indermark, John, 1950–
    The greatest of these : biblical moorings of love / John Indermark.
        p.   cm.
    ISBN 978-1-4267-3090-0 (trade pbk. : alk. paper)
    1. Love—Biblical teaching.   I. Title.
    BS680.L64I53   2011
    241'.4—dc22

                                                                    2011011690

11 12 13 14 15 16 17 18 19 20—10 9 8 7 6 5 4 3 2 1

MANUFACTURED IN THE UNITED STATES OF AMERICA

To
Judy and Jeff

For love's gift
and family's joy

CONTENTS

Acknowledgments vii

Introduction ix

1. Love as Gift 1

2. Love as Invitation 21

3. Love as Loyalty 41

4. Love as Ethic 61

5. Love as Compassion 81

6. Love as Wonder 101

Leader's Guide 119

ACKNOWLEDGMENTS

The origin of the title for *The Greatest of These* was singular, borrowing Paul's memorable phrase that closes 1 Corinthians 13 and its elevation of love above all God's gifts. But the origin of the material contained between these covers, not to mention how these stories came to take on printed form, is multiple. And multiple acknowledgments of thanks are in order.

I owe thanks for the mooring of faith in love to the teachers who nurtured that connection in the Sunday school of Salvator Evangelical and Reformed Church in St. Louis. Two women in particular stand out in my memory: Mrs. Ada Prell, superintendent of the Kindergarten Department and wife of the pastor who confirmed me; and Mrs. Lillian Schaefer, superintendent of the Primary Department and the first person who suggested I should be a minister. As one of the readings will unpack more fully, their ingraining us in song and word that "God is love" made an indelible impression on me and countless others. As I grew, I also came to see that what these two women taught was what they lived. My parents and grandparents provided me with unconditional love, and that experience has strongly shaped the perspectives on love you will find in these pages. I am also deeply grateful to the editors and designers at The United Methodist Publishing House, for their contributions to the book.

Finally, I gladly acknowledge my thanks to my wife and partner, Judy, and our son, Jeff. In the end, love requires embodiment. The presence and love of these two have shaped me in ways that exceed my words, and have made it possible for me to practice a ministry of writing all these years.

INTRODUCTION

Why This Book?

The time in the worship service comes for the pastor's "children's sermon." During this time, the pastor often asks a question. I have noticed that children most frequently offer two answers, whether or not they directly relate to the pastor's question: "Jesus" or "love." These answers may partly stem from a tendency of children's sermons to boil down to one of those two themes. The answers also emerge from those two themes, which provide the core identity and vocation for Christian community. You cannot have Christian community without taking Jesus into account. And you cannot have Christian community without taking love into account.

The Greatest of These: Biblical Moorings of Love explores the meaning and practice of love in Christian faith. As children's sermons reveal, the theme of love serves as a catch-all of Christian faith. Love offers a watchword and a byword among us—but what do we mean by *love*? What exactly is it we are suggesting when we invoke cherished affirmations like "God is love" or "love one another"? This book will invite readers and study groups to delve deeply and intentionally into what the biblical witness has to say about love—and what that implies for how we practice love.

Notice I said "biblical witness" and not simply "New Testament." Sometimes the church proceeds as if "love" shows up only when Jesus comes along. That outlook is perilous in both its one-sided depiction of Judaism and its negligence of how Christian teaching on love grows out of our Jewish roots. Each chapter in this book will explore a particular theme of love through six biblical passages: one each from Torah, Prophets, and Writings (Old Testament); and one each from Gospels, Pauline Epistles, and General Epistles (New Testament).

A Lexicon on Love

The languages of the Bible, Old Testament Hebrew and New Testament Greek, provide intriguing insights into what is and is not meant by *love* in the biblical works.

Four Greek words in use during New Testament times for various kinds of love are: *eros, philos, storge,* and *agape*. *Eros*, like its English derivative *erotic*, has chiefly to do with intense desire. While it can refer to the desire for that which is true and good, it has been associated most frequently with sensuality and sexuality. *Eros* does not appear in any New Testament text. *Philos* is love primarily associated with friendship. It occurs a number of times in the New Testament, primarily in contexts where the love spoken of is between individuals or in community. *Storge* refers to familial love and occurs in combination with *philos* in Romans 12:10. In Romans 12, Paul uses variations of *agape, philos,* and *storge* in the instructions for relating to one another as members of the body of Christ. *Agape*, as used by Christians, refers to the self-giving love that is given by God. In the New Testament, variations of this word are used in reference to God's love for humankind, individually or collectively. *Agape* suggests the unconditional love that finds illustration in Jesus' command to his disciples: "Love one another . . . *as I have loved you*" (John 13:34, italics added). For the community of Jesus Christ, *agape* comes to us not by our earning or demanding it, but by the sheer grace of God's self-giving love. Jesus calls his followers to this same, self-giving love offered to us by God.

Ahav, racham, and *hesed* are Hebrew word roots translated as various kinds of love in the Old Testament. *Ahav* carries a variety of meanings, including "to breathe after," or long for, something, "to love," and "to delight in." *Racham* carries the primary sense of compassion. *Hesed*, often translated as *steadfast love* or *loving kindness*, suggests zeal and passion along with kindness, mercy, pity, and benevolence. It denotes the fierce loyalty of God to covenant, a persistent willingness to go the extra mile for the sake of covenant and community. Love as *hesed* brings "stick-to-it-iveness" into love's meaning and practice, even as it forms the essence of God's character and action.

Using This Book

The Greatest of These is intended to be read over a six-week period, one chapter per week. Each chapter has six daily readings on one of the themes noted earlier, prefaced by a one-page introduction to the chapter theme. If you are using this book in a weekly group study, pace your readings so that you do one reading per day, with the group meeting on the seventh day. If you are reading this as an individual study or devotional guide, follow the pattern of one reading per day. Use the seventh day of each week as a "sabbath" to reflect on the past week's readings.

Each daily reading consists of a title, a Scripture reference, a reading that grows out of that passage, and a brief prayer or spiritual exercise. Please read the Scripture passage first. It sets the stage for the reading that follows. Allow time to linger over the prayer or spiritual exercise. These exercises are designed to bring each reading into deeper connection with your personal spiritual journey. You will find space to write about insights you gain from the reading or from the exercise. If you will be leading or assisting a group study of this book (or if you are just curious!), you will find a leader guide at the end of the book with suggestions and discussion questions for group sessions. For individuals using this book alone, these might serve as a guide for "sabbath" reflection on each chapter.

Blessings on your journey with this book as companion. Led by God's Spirit, alone or in company with others, may your exploration of love's meaning empower your practice of love's vocation!

John Indermark

chapter 1

LOVE AS GIFT

The inauguration of Barack Obama on January 20, 2009, included a quartet performing a John Williams arrangement of "Air and Simple Gifts." "Simple Gifts" comes from the Shaker tradition, and its tune is likely just as familiar as its opening words: " 'Tis the gift to be simple, 'tis the gift to be free." Those themes ran deep in that day's celebration of new beginnings. The opening line of another verse set to that same tune and song is: " 'Tis the gift to be loved, and that love to return." These words resonate with the purpose of the opening chapter in this book on love.

To know ourselves loved—and loved by God—is an extraordinary gift. It provides a powerful and enduring foundation upon which to build our lives in joyful response to that gift. *The Greatest of These* begins its exploration of love's meaning and practice in the biblical witness through the prism of love as gift. This chapter views love as gift from a variety of angles: as foundation and companion; in gracious choice and purposeful working; through reflecting on who God is; and in embracing who we may come to be. The knowledge that God loves us serves as the bedrock of our faith formation and our discipleship.

FOUNDATIONS   JOHN 3:16-17

I am hard-pressed to remember the gifts I received when I graduated from college back in 1972, but one gift stays not only in my mind but in my library. It is a Bible presented to me by a couple from my home church, Fay and Len. I am grateful for all that they gave to me throughout my youth and young adulthood. Fay taught the youth and young adult class I had been part of during high school and university years. Len served on the church council and played regularly at the church's Monday night volleyball sessions where I spent considerable time as a youth. Their daughter Bev was one of my best friends through all those years. So what has all of this to do with a book on love and a reading entitled "Foundations"? On the inside front cover of the Bible, after words of congratulation and blessing, they inscribed this: "Remember, God so loved John Indermark that He gave . . ."

Many view John 3:16-17 as *the* foundational statement for Christian theology. Billy Graham is reported to have said that all of his sermons come down to these pivotal words of Jesus to Nicodemus. It is natural for these familiar words to begin this chapter in a book devoted to the exploration of love. Their familiarity challenges us to hear these words with freshness and in a way that allows them to shape our understanding and practice of love as gift.

Love arises first of all from God: "For *God* so loved" (italics added). The initiative to love is God's. Nothing here depicts God's love as either beckoned or badgered into being by us. God loves without any precondition outside of God's own will to love. That is a word the church sorely needs to hear anew when we get caught up in cycles of judgment that draw increasingly restricted circles around the ones we deem to merit such love. That is a word we all need to hear when we fall prey to doubts about the lovability or acceptability of others—or ourselves—in the eyes of God. The foundation of love as gift is first of all that God's love trumps any self-justifying posturing or self-hating humiliation. We start out loved because that is who God is and what God does.

What is the object of God's love? "For God so loved *the world*" (italics added). The assertion of a world beloved of God is not an innovation of John or even Jesus. The creation story of Genesis 1 employs two re-peated refrains in its liturgy of beginnings: "and God said" and "it was good." God deems the world to be good at the outset, a deeming affirmed by John 3:16-17. God is not a world-hater. The God of John 3:16-17 loves this world with a very specific purpose and intent: God in Christ came not to condemn but to *save* the world. The verse does not say that the target of God's saving is the church. The verse does not say that the targets of God's saving are those who have the same religious or political views as I do. The world that God in Genesis deemed good is the same world God re-deems, as in deems good again, with love. The foundation of love as gift is, second, that God's love and saving purposes are aimed at the whole God-loved world.

Yet love that is as broad as all creation is also by nature focused on particular individuals. That is what the inscription on the front of my graduation Bible from Len and Fay conveys to me. God does not love in generalities or in the abstract. At some point, love must become personal. For Nicodemus. For me. For you. We fail to grasp the extraordinary breadth and depth of God's love if we do not accept ourselves—and oth-ers—as particular individuals whom God loves and with whom God seeks loving relationship. That, to me, ties into the emphasis on belief in verse 16. The world-saving love of God seeks our active trust and fol-lowing. The foundation of love as gift, third, relies on our engaging God's love for us with personal trust.

Finally, the focus of love's trust, even as the nature of love's gift, is not a "what" but a "who." The Son. The Beloved. The Christ. Whatever metaphor of identity we choose, the love of God comes to the world in the God-given One. So finally, the foundation of love as gift comes in the mystery of God's love incarnate. This means, among other things, that when we speak of love, we can never afford to do so in purely spiritual or abstract terms. The foundation of love as gift, upon which we build our faith, relies on love taking on the most human and humane of forms. God's love precedes our own. God's love embraces the whole world, fashioning communities and focusing upon each individual. God's love beckons our trust. God's love comes to us in the person of Jesus. God's love then seeks our embodiment of its gift. These are the foundations upon which love is built. These are the foundations from which this book begins its journey, and invites your own, into love's meaning and call.

Say aloud, "for God so loved [your name]." What do you trust those words to mean in your life? What do they invite you to be and do? Say aloud, "for God so loved the world." Reflect on those same questions in regards to God's love for the world.

Named and Companioned   Isaiah 43:1-7

*No matter what happens, we are going to be with you through this, and
we are going to come out together on the other side.* Those are not the exact
words, but they are the spirit of what my wife and I told our son not too
many years ago when he was experiencing a cascading descent of health
issues. We could not promise instant healing. We could not alleviate what
he was going through. But we were bound and determined to be with
him, to be companions as best we were able, through some very rough
and frightening times. More than once, we spoke his name in the midst
of those assurances, not to get his attention, but to underscore his belonging to the love that first named him at birth and now would be with
him through this time.

I suppose we said such things and sought to offer such companionship out of having received similar support and the gift of love's
presence in our own lives. In my life, that support and presence has
been mediated through a variety of persons and communities. I remember particularly the evening of our son's birth. We planned that I
would be with Judy in the delivery room, and for much of the day I was
with her. But a problem developed that required a C-section. These
being the days before fathers could remain in the room for such proce-
dures, I was gently but firmly informed that I needed to leave. So much
for well-laid plans.

Much of the day, people from our church in that small community had
been dropping by to see how things were going. Word spread quickly of
a problem. By the time I had to leave Judy and walk out into the tiny re-
ception area in a not-so-great emotional state brought on by the disappointment and swirl of events, a dozen or more members of the church
were there in the waiting room. One woman had even smuggled in
homemade potato soup for me to eat. In that moment, I suddenly found
myself companioned by the community that I was supposed to serve as
minister. Through their companionship, they ministered to me. They

5

walked with me through the next few hours, and they celebrated when I brought out our newly birthed son.

When I read Isaiah 43:1-7, I have two sets of lenses. I read with the lens of biblical background nurtured in me by Sunday school teachers all the way through seminary professors. I also read with the lens of my personal faith and experience of God.

Isaiah 43:1-7 tells the news that Israel's promised release from captivity and exile will not be an everyone-for-themselves breakout. Release and homecoming will be made possible by the promise of God's companionship. "I will be with you," God declares (v. 2). What makes that offer of companionship so *vital*, in the literal, life-giving sense of that word's meaning, is that the One who will be with them is the One who first gave them life in creation, the God "who created you" and "who formed you" (vv. 1, 7). Their companion will be the Holy One who called them by name, the first gift of a parent to a child brought into life (v. 1). The passage surely is a story of power, of the God who creates and redeems and saves. But the passage is also a story of love, where power is exercised for the sake of those beloved by God and where love's power comes precisely in this gift of companionship. "Do not fear . . . I will be with you" (vv. 1, 2).

That theme of companionship leads to the second set of lenses with which I read this passage, provided by the experience of knowing myself the beneficiary of companionship and love—and if beneficiary, then called to be agent of companionship and love. In my biased perspective, none of us can truly read—much less understand—the promises and calls of faith without this second set of lenses. God gifts our lives by naming us as beloved, as symbolized in the liturgy of baptism. God promises to companion us as God's new creation—and to empower us by God's Spirit to exercise love's gifts toward others.

Why would companionship, the gift of presence, be so important as to be considered an act of God-expressing love? From my pastoral experience, sometimes the most important thing I could do—sometimes, the *only* thing I could do—was to be with someone. At a bedside. In a hospital. In a courtroom. But what is it about companionship that makes it such a gift? Think for a moment about the very word: *com-panion*. The prefix "com-" brings the sense of "together" or "with." And "-panion"? It derives from the Latin word for "bread." A companion is one who shares bread, the most basic of ancient foods. Spiritually speaking, "companions" are those who share the bread of relationship, whose presence "feeds" our deep needs for belonging and connection. Spiritually speaking, "companions" are those through whom God's Spirit "feeds" our faith and nurtures our spirits, who bear to us the presence of God through their presence.

In Isaiah 43, God promises to be our companion. Come water or fire, river or flame, God will be with us. That is love's gift to the ancient people of Israel in exile; that is love's gift to those today who wonder if anyone cares or remembers: to be loved and companioned by God who calls us by name. For that reason, Isaiah declares not once but twice: "do not fear" (vv. 1, 5). Why? *No matter what happens, I am going to be with you through this, and we are going to come out together on the other side.*

Identify someone in your community who at this moment is in need of a "companion." What are some ways you can companion that individual? How might God's companioning of you give you the strength and courage to serve as that companion?

GRACIOUS CHOICES   DEUTERONOMY 7:7-9

Why me? Imagine the ways and situations in which those words may be invoked. At times, they rise up in complaint, faithful or otherwise, that ponder why some ill has befallen you or those you love. A doctor intones that the cancer test has come back positive. A supervisor informs that cutbacks had to be made and that you are the one. At other times, these words may arise out of the wonder of something that has surprisingly and perhaps undeservedly come your way for your good. A parent, or a child, or a partner, extends words of acceptance and forgiveness in a situation where you might have expected or warranted their rejection and resentment. An individual reflects on life and dwells more on its blessings than its hurdles. *Why me?*

The experience of love as gift brings the question *why me?* to the fore. For most of us, excluding those who have such inflated opinions of themselves that they cannot imagine anyone *not* loving them, love engenders serious reflection on *why me?* as we consider how and why the beloved graces our lives. It is no less so when the love extended our direction is that of God. *Why me?* offers an apt response to the amazement of considering ourselves loved by the God whose wisdom and power could have opted for any number of ways to relate to us. Yet the relationship chosen by God was love, and we were the ones graciously chosen. Care needs to be taken at just this point, lest we make of *why me?* a laundry list of self-congratulation rather than a sense of wonder at love as gift and gracious choice. Our passage from Deuteronomy, and its wider context in the whole of this book, sheds critical light on this matter.

Deuteronomy addressed the people of Israel, who were poised to enter the land of promise. Deuteronomy was thus set not only in the wake of Israel's deliverance from Egypt by God; its setting was the aftermath of the people's murmurings against leaders and against God, who had seemingly led them out into the wilderness to die. Its setting was the aftermath of the people's longing to be back in slavery in Egypt, where at least their bellies were full (Exodus 14:11-12; 16:3). The setting was after the people had fashioned a golden calf in direct violation of the commandment against making idols (Exodus 20:4). Its setting was the aftermath of years of wandering that brought an entirely new generation to the edge of the land.

In spite of all that background, Deuteronomy 7:7-9 proclaims God's gracious choice of Israel. Even with that history of recalcitrance, some might have been tempted to think that their being chosen by God resulted from something other than grace. In other words, some may have thought about God's choosing not as *why me?* but as a prideful *who else could it have been?* "It was not because you were more numerous than any other people" is how verse 7 binds the choice to God's grace. The Hebrew word translated as "numerous" also connotes "abundance." It is not Israel's impressiveness in numbers or prestige or wealth, or whatever "stuff" we may claim, that sways God. Rather, the choice resides solely in the disposition of God's heart.

Consider then the faith by which we understand ourselves and others as chosen of God. Whenever those understandings or claims veer away from the gracious disposition of God's heart and move into the assertion of our being chosen because we are more _____ (you fill in the blank) than others, we dismiss accepting grace on its own terms. Deuteronomy 7:7 closes by reasserting the gracious character of God's choice: "for you were the *fewest* of all peoples" (italics added).

Identifying the choice of Israel by God, even though they were the *fewest* of all, asserts a humbling yet liberating dynamic. For love to be love—whether of God for us, or us for one another—grace rather than reciprocity (*you scratch my back and I'll scratch yours*) must be at its core. Deuteronomy's portrayal of God's love for and choosing of the "fewest" anticipates one of Jesus' more radical teachings: "Just as you did it to one of the *least* of these who are members of my family, you did it to me" (Matthew 25:40, italics added). The *fewest* and the *least* reveal the gracious character of God's choice of love in Deuteronomy and Christ's call to love in Matthew.

I suppose such choices and calls could evoke bewilderment at *why them?* But where God invites us to begin is in the disarming realization of *why me?* For once we accept ourselves as God loves and accepts us, the path opens for us to accept and love others on that same basis of radical and gracious acceptance.

Open my heart, O God, to your heart, that I may accept its
    gracious gift:
your choice to love me and to love all. In Jesus Christ. Amen.

"Things Work Together for Good"   Romans 8:28

We drove from eastern Washington to a growing community outside Seattle. Rain accompanied us most of the trip. We were driving to a church where I was a candidate for pastor. As we neared the town where it was located, the skies brightened and a rainbow appeared. I remarked to my wife that this must mean something. That Sunday, I accepted the call to serve as their pastor.

Within a year, the situation deteriorated into a serious mismatch. My conference minister encouraged me to hang tough. As time passed, *hang* became the operative word for me. The church and I mutually agreed on my departure. Had anyone asked then, I would have expressed sincere doubts about the wisdom of Paul's words about all things working together for good.

What do I say now? If my relationship with that congregation had not suffered meltdown, I may not have considered coming to the town of Naselle that has been home for twenty-seven years. If I had not come here, I might not have had the time or opportunity to seriously contemplate, much less to actively pursue, a ministry of writing. If I had not sought to expand my ministry of the written word while keeping one foot in the parish door, I might not have been drawn to accept part-time supply and interim ministries in Lutheran and Presbyterian and United Methodist congregations in southwest Washington and northwest Oregon that have made ecumenism less a principle and more a given in my life and ministry.

We know that all things work together *for good.* Sometimes, the working together takes longer than we would like. Sometimes, the working together takes a different form than we would have envisioned. At my ordination in 1976, I had an extremely clear idea of what the "good" of my ministry would look like, and where it would be practiced: full-time pastoring in churches of the United Church of Christ. Things change. Nineteen years have passed since either of those conditions has been the case. But good has come that I would not exchange.

All things can work together for good. I say "can," for Paul himself qualifies the statement with "for those who love God." When self-interest or maintaining privileged positions of power go unchecked by love, when we are obsessed with making sure all things go our predetermined way regardless of consequences for others or ourselves, we are apt to pull our individual threads out of the weave God would fashion of our lives. To act on the basis of love toward God and toward one another opens our lives and ways to the purposes of God. In such openings, through such purposes, things and persons can work together for good, whether it is the good expected all along or the good that surprises with its unexpected but grace-filled twists.

Grace-filled twists return us to this chapter's theme of love as gift. Paul links the working together of all things for good for those who love God. Make no mistake: the reason such disparate and even contradictory experiences in our lives can eventually work together for good arises out of God's love for us. As I read Scripture and as I read the hieroglyphs of my own experience, God's love working for good in human life does not wait for us to love first, as if we alone must trigger God's working for our good.

Take, for an example, Paul, also known by the Hebrew name of Saul. I would be hard-pressed to make a case for Saul's love of God when, as a young man, he looked after the coats of those who rained down stones upon Stephen until the church's first martyr lay bloody and dead. Acts 8:1 states Saul's approval of this murder. I see no love of God in Saul "still breathing threats and murder" as he rounds up followers of Jesus for arrest (Acts 9:1) But God works in all these things: in a flashing light, by a stroke of blindness, through an initially reluctant Ananias (Acts 9). God works through all these things together to bring about good. Saul experiences conversion and uses his zeal to bring others to Jesus.

The gift of Romans 8:28 is that the working together of all things—even the things that in and of themselves bear ill will toward us or others, even the things we do not see or understand, even the things we would not have chosen or expected—will eventuate in good. It will be so, not because each and every occurrence in our lives or the life of this world is good. It will be so, not even because each and every occurrence in our lives or the life of this world is an act of God. It will be so, because God is good. For God is love.

Think of a good that has come to you in your life of late. Perhaps it is something in your church life or spiritual journey. Perhaps it is in a personal relationship. Now, as best as you are able, trace backward how it came to be. Pay attention to the people who made it possible. Give thanks for them. Call to mind the stages or "preparations" where "one thing led to another." Give thanks for that confluence of situations and developments and opportunities—for doors closed as well as doors opened that led to this. Finally, give thanks to God for the mystery—or clarity—of God's working through these things. Think now of a situation you are facing that is unclear, where the "good" is uncertain. Seek God's guidance and trust in the working of God's good.

"God Is Love"   1 John 4:16

It is an odd thing the way memories of early childhood can linger for decades. Sometimes memories are summoned by a sound. Sometimes they sneak up on us unannounced, catching us by surprise as we wonder in our later adulthood why and how that bit of experience not recalled for years comes flooding through in powerful ways. Sometimes, though, they are like familiar and trusted companions. Their recollection has been steady through the years, and their effect upon us can be profound.

Such a memory comes to me from my Sunday mornings in what I recall to have been the lower primary department of Salvator Evangelical and Reformed Church. The setting was the church gymnasium that served as our gathering place before heading off to individual classes. Some aspects of that place were a bit odd. The gymnasium, built below ground, had a series of windows running lengthwise along the ceiling on the western wall. Light literally came from on high through those windows to pour upon us children seated in our miniature chairs.

The part of the memory that connects to this book and this chapter on love as gift has to do with a song I am sure I sang most every week in those early years. I doubt if I ever saw the words, as I imagine they were learned by rote. But they still come to mind with ease fifty and more years after the last time my voice joined with other children. The pastor's wife, Mrs. Prell, led the song: *Praise him, praise him, all ye little children: God is love, God is love. Praise him, praise him, all ye little children, God is love, God is love.* As I recall, sometimes we repeated the chorus, substituting "serve" or "love" for "praise." But what was underlying, what was bedrock to us, was this recurring phrase: *God is love, God is love.*

A cynic might charge that the minds of little ones were being brainwashed by subliminal repetition. *God is love, God is love.* If that were the case, thank Mrs. Prell and thank God. I have since forgotten all the flannel board stories. The little craft projects we made quickly found their way into wastebaskets. The words of this childhood song and its core message, however, endured. *God is love, God is love.*

I once shared this story in a sermon offered at a nearby Presbyterian church, whose pulpit I filled during their pastoral search. When it came to conveying the words of the chorus, I did not say them, but sang them. The reaction on some people's faces was fascinating. It was a mixture of recognition and gladness. I don't know whether the recognition was of this particular chorus, or the triggered memory of one like it that they have carried with them for as many and perhaps more years than I have. I suspect the gladness came from getting reacquainted with a companion of theirs, words that have deeply informed their faith even though they may not have been at the front of the mind or on the tip of the tongue for some time. *God is love, God is love.*

I share this memory and story here because the simple words of this chorus have conveyed to me for over half a century the foundation of God's love as gift. As years pass, as responsibilities grow, as lives and theologies get more complicated, I find rest and peace in knowing that some things are more deeply true and more enduring than we little children ever suspected. *God is love, God is love.* Our lives are grounded in the simple yet profound message that "God is love," a gift celebrated not only by 1 John 4:16 but also by the Salvator Evangelical and Reformed Church primary department chorus.

So what is the enduring value of such a simple gift that takes hold deep inside us? Several years back, I was asked to offer the eulogy for Slim, a former logger, neighbor, and jack-of-all-trades when it came to getting things fixed or done at the parsonage. His wife, Helen, had, by the time of Slim's death, slipped under the veil of some form of dementia. As I spoke about Slim, I could only hope that there was something she heard that comforted, that stirred memory of his life and their partnership over the years. I ended the eulogy with the Lord's Prayer. And that's when it happened. Helen, who had been silent throughout the service, suddenly raised her voice and spoke so loudly she led the congregation in that prayer. Whether she heard anything I had said mattered little. That prayer's words tapped deeper than the dementia.

Maybe, just maybe, that is the kind of hope and enduring gift that the teachers of our primary chorus had in mind for us as well, that we might have words to live by and to fall back on when all other words failed. That we might have love to fall back on when other loves seemed out of our reach or awareness. That we might have words to remind us in the depths of our being that all is well and all will be well: *God is love, God is love*—all ye little children, God is love.

What are the deep and abiding memories, along with the stirring thoughts and hopes, that remind you that God's gift to you is love?

"My Times Are in Your Hand"   Psalm 31:14-16

When, and why, have you placed yourself in another's hands? Sometimes the decision arises from physical need. Your doctor counsels that surgery is needed, or chemotherapy is required. You trust her judgment, and place yourself in her hands.

Sometimes the decision emerges from the realization of emotional longings and love's tidal surges. You stand next to the beloved and in the presence of witnesses offer words of promise and commitment. You entrust yourself and who you will become and what you will do together into his hands, and he into yours.

Sometimes the decision is less a decision and more of a trusting movement. Can you remember as a child reaching a hand up to cross a street, to walk into a doctor's office, or perhaps with no apparent reason other than the need or joy of having someone hold on to you? Or, have you been the one to whom a child has reached out in trust and openness to what your hand offered in that moment?

It is not always an easy thing to place who we are and who we may yet become into another's hand. There is a sense of vulnerability in the act. That helps explain why the one consistent piece of information in each of the scenarios described above, and perhaps the ones they evoked from your own experiences, is trust. We do not usually place ourselves in the hands of those we do not trust, or who have given us cause to think or imagine they will do us ill. That is one reason why the betrayal of those who place themselves in the hands of a heretofore trusted figure is so outrageous. When the trusted one preys upon the vulnerabilities of those who come seeking a helping rather than a harming hand, they do far more damage than whatever the physical or financial abuse may be. They abuse power entrusted to them.

In Hebrew, the word for "hand" can also be translated as "power." To be in another's hands is to be in another's power. So hear the psalmist's cry and our own cries for help in that same light. To place ourselves in

God's hand is a transaction that bids God's power to hold us. That can be a comforting word in our times of powerlessness. That can also be a charged word in the face of powers that have other purposes for us and for our times than our good.

The psalmist confesses to God: "my times are in your hand." When the whole of Psalm 31 is read, it becomes clear that this particular phrase is no formulaic recital of expected piety. The psalm veers back and forth between acknowledgments of trust and laments of adversity. The times reflected in the psalmist's experience are a bewildering combination that lifts affirmations of God as rock as well as a "life . . . spent with sorrow" and "my years with sighing." Yet the psalmist does not resign himself to fate or unjust circumstances. The psalmist places all these times in God's hand, in hope of God's saving by "steadfast love."

God's "steadfast love." That word in Hebrew, *hesed*, expresses intense and zealous love, kindness, and mercy. God's *hesed* is the steadfast love that goes the extra mile for the sake of Israel and for our sake. *Hesed* is the foundation of persistent, enduring love that comes as gift from God.

The hand into which the psalmist places his times is extended in *hesed*, God's steadfast love that will not let us go. Such a hand, such a love, such a power is broad and persistent enough to hold on through such times as confessed by the psalmist and by us. Such love can be trusted, for God's power can be trusted for our good and the good of all.

As this initial chapter on love as gift draws to a close, be mindful of and grateful for the gift this psalm extends: the gift that we may place our times, the whole of our lives, into the hands of God. For those hands, while powerful, are good. They are hands cupped in steadfast and persistent love for our keeping and the keeping of all creation. They are hands that beckon our trust and summon our own practice of love both gracious and persistent.

"My times are in your hand." Use the phrase as the repeating line of a litany. Consider the times when you have felt closest to God, when faith and love have been clear. Name them, and pray: "My times are in your hand." Consider times filled with difficulty, or doubt, or fear. Name them, and pray: "My times are in your hand." Consider the times most immediate to your life and faith at this moment. Name them, and pray: "My times are in your hand." Consider the times that lie ahead, that stretch beyond your knowledge and perhaps even your imagination. Pray: "My times are in your hand."

chapter 2

LOVE AS INVITATION

Invitations. We have all received them during the course of our lives. As children, we may have received invitations to birthday parties. As adults, we may have received invitations to weddings or open houses or graduations. Invitations may solicit our presence at a celebration. Invitations may beckon our participation in some event. Invitations may lift us up because they affirm that we are included in something beyond ourselves. Invitations may put us on the spot because we must decide whether to respond to a stated or implied R.S.V.P. (*repondez, s'il vous plait*—"respond, if you please").

Love in the biblical witness and in the life of faith comes to us as an open-ended invitation. Such love bears its own requests to "R.S.V.P." This chapter will tap into the possibilities of our responses to love's invitation: to move out of self toward God and other; to provoke one another to love; to choose specific actions for good; to keep and endure in love; to practice love out of enlightened self-interest; and to hold together love's telling with love's showing. Building upon the foundation of love as gift, love as invitation calls upon us to make that love our own, to receive it from God, and to practice it in our lives.

"Arise"   Song of Solomon 2:8-13

If you have not read the passage indicated above, stop right now and do so. Are you wondering what an unabashed love poem is doing here? If you think this passage may just be an aberration, an unfair lifting of a text out of context, feel free to read the rest of Song of Solomon. The book is love poetry, plain and simple.

Though actually, it is not so simple. Readers and scholars have debated the inclusion of this work in Scripture for a very long time. The second-century Rabbi Aqiba warned his contemporaries that "he who trills his voice in chanting the Song of Songs in the banquet house and treats it as a sort of song has no part in the world to come"[1] Love poetry, erotic poetry, can certainly raise eyebrows, whether in second-century Judaism or twenty-first-century Christianity. Such language and imagery as Song of Solomon engages in pushes the edge of PG-13 ratings for readings suitable for children. So why did it land in the Bible—especially since this book does not once mention God, a dubious distinction shared only with the Book of Esther? Esther, at least, bears direct ties to the liturgical life of Judaism by telling the origin of *Purim*. What does Song of Solomon have going for it?

Love. The Song of Solomon employs the imagery of human passion and love. It may be that its eroticism came to be accepted into the canon of Scripture because some interpreted this imagery as a metaphor or allegory of God's love for Israel—or later, of Christ's love for the church. But those are meanings that have been placed upon the text from outside. Read it from the inside, and you read the poetry of love and sensuality.

Two other unique aspects mark this biblical work. First, you primarily hear the voice of an unnamed female character. Second, the woman whose voice carries most of the narrative is black (Song of Solomon 1:5). Translators over time have sometimes tried to "soften" that self-description of the woman, using all sorts of euphemisms for who knows what motives.

But as noted in *The New Interpreter's Bible* commentary, the Hebrew word translated as "black" is unambiguous in its meaning[2]—even as the whole book is unambiguous in its focus upon love.

The passage out of which this reading arises begins with the voice of this woman marking the approach of her beloved. But then, the sound of the beloved's approach gives way to his voice of invitation: "Arise, my love, my fair one, and come away" (v. 10). The exact phrase appears again at the end of verse 13, with this repeated invitation bracketing an elegant announcement that springtime has come. The beloved invites his partner to "arise . . . and come away."

Love involves invitation, and the invitation inevitably brings movement of some sort or another. In more traditional biblical passages, the invitation to love, whether of God or neighbor or the stranger among us, often bids movement away from self-absorption so that love for the other can be expressed. The love poetry in Song of Solomon mirrors that same invitation. Only now, the arena is the intimacy of human relationship and the longing for the beloved to join with the partner. Again, some speculate that this poetry in Song of Solomon arose out of a desire to portray the covenantal relationship between God and Israel. Others speculate as to whether the attraction of religious covenant drew upon a more primal longing to be with another in this world. Either way, truth is told. For love to be love, solitude must at times be set aside for companionship and partnership. Love is not fulfilled by two who stand still and go nowhere. Love brings the invitation: "arise . . . come away."

Individuals and churches, bid by God's love to engage in love, at times prefer standing still, if not retreating. When times grow difficult, we may feel as if there are no new seasons before us anymore, that our better days are behind us. We may shut out all voices, save the ones that reinforce our cynicism. Perhaps that is why some give up on this world and hope only for the next. In contrast, Song of Solomon invites opening to love's life-making possibilities in the present moment, the immediacy of "now."

"Arise . . . come away." Love always beckons to new places. It does so, in the imagery of this passage, with the promise of spring, where rains have ended and flowers appear and nature goes into its bloom again. Love in our faith's journey invites such movement. Love beckons us to open to the One whose approach assures the promise of new seasons of growth in our lives and communities. Love entices us with the surprise at what seemed to be only dry, dead vines suddenly leafing out and setting forth fruit. Love pleads for us to receive the vow that life can be more than it has been. Love invites us not only to think and hope such things but to take the risk to live and speak and act on those hopes.

Arise, my love . . . arise, *for* love.

In what ways do your experiences of the intimacy of human love shed light on how you perceive and experience God's love— and God's invitation to practice love? Offer a prayer for your spiritual journey that grows out of the language of Song of Solomon 2:8-13.

"PROVOKE ONE ANOTHER TO LOVE"   HEBREWS 10:23-25

At first glance, the title of this reading and its urging in verse 24 to "provoke one another to love" seems a bit odd. What do you typically associate with "provoking" someone—or someone provoking you? Anger? Frustration? Throwing someone, or having another throw you, off guard? Raising your blood pressure? *Don't provoke me* sounds less like a rejection of love's invitation and more an effort to avoid love's opposite. So why speak of provoking one another to love?

Years ago, there was a student in my seminary class who I will call Bill. If there was anyone more quiet or reserved than me in the class, it would have been Bill. You wouldn't think of it to look at him. He had the physique of a tight end on a football team. But he was a gentle spirit. During our second year, Bill did his practicum of field work in a Clinical Pastoral Education program at a local hospital. Part of the program involved regular group sessions with other C.P.E. students and their leader. Those sessions were not merely times to report on their visits among the patients but opportunities to explore issues of personal and religious dynamics triggered by those experiences for the sake of deepening professional and spiritual growth.

One day, in another class, Bill asked if he might share an experience that had occurred to him in his C.P.E. program. Bill told us that in one of the C.P.E. group gatherings, the leader kept provoking him, as he did frequently when the group gathered. On one particular day, the leader's provocation finally pushed Bill over the edge. Bill said the next thing he knew, he had physically lifted up and pinned the leader against the wall. At that moment, the leader spoke to him and congratulated him for finally letting go of trying to be in such control of his emotions that he never risked vulnerability. My first thought after hearing the story was that Bill should have throttled the guy for playing mind games. But Bill was sincerely grateful and sincerely changed. In his heart, he had been provoked for the good.

When do we provoke others, and ourselves, to love? Dr. Fred Craddock, as he comments on this verse in *The New Interpreter's Bible*, makes this helpful observation about the positive sense of *provoke*: "disturbing the apathetic or fearful person into activity."[3] Individuals and communities who are already engaged and immersed in actions of love and good generally need encouragement or support, not provoking, to go about such work. To provoke, as Craddock suggests, aims more in the direction of persons and places where inertia has taken hold, where the risk of where and to whom love might take us pulls the reins and digs in the heels. Love is not always and everywhere synonymous with sentiments printed by Hallmark. Love may invite us to stand with victims of HIV-AIDS. Love may invite us to open our doors to those who routinely have had doors closed upon them. Love may invite us to church life that is not only potlucks and friendly greeters and great music but solidarity with the least and the lowly. For in them, Christ astounds if not scandalizes us by meeting us in *their* person.

We may need to provoke such exercise of love in our midst from time to time. Fear and apathy can cause love's invitation to remain unheard under their shouted din of *keep it safe* or *don't get involved*. The link between love's provocation and hearing love's invitation can be seen in the key verb in Hebrews 10:24. The word chosen to render this Greek verb in Hebrews is *provoke*. Consider the two roots that combine to make this verb. The first root is "pro," a prefix that can mean "in favor of" or "to direct action toward" something. The second root is "vocare," which means "to call." This same root is also in the word *vocation*, a word that Christians often refer to as "calling." Our most fundamental vocation, or calling, as followers of Jesus is to love. To love God. To love neighbor, which includes the stranger. To love ourselves. That's what Jesus told us, anyway, in his identification of the "greatest" commandment.

Seen in this way, to "provoke" someone to love—and that someone should include one's self—means to urge another to reclaim and jump-start the God-given and God-graced vocation to love. It is a vocation we are most inclined to set aside in times of fear, in moments of indifference, and in the lullaby that comfort-seeking affluence can sing. In all such times, when our vocation to love is set aside, the season is open to provoke one another to love.

Perhaps such provocation can be accomplished in ways not quite so confrontational as my fellow seminarian Bill experienced. But sometimes, love's invitation may require a rude awakening to the truth that love is not one option among many on some spiritual buffet table from which we may pick and choose whatever pleases us. Love is the main course: for love is God's pleasure made incarnate for our sake, and love is the vocation with which God is most pleased. "Provoke one another to love."

Where are the places in your life where "provocation" of love might be in order? Reflect on the same question in regard to your congregation. And now, how will you respond to the call to provoke one another to love? Pray about it. And as you are able, provoke it!

For the Good of . . .   Amos 5:14-15

For the good of . . . How have you heard, and how have you spoken, a completion of that phrase? In political seasons and settings, "for the good of the *country*" or "for the good of the *party*" come into play, oftentimes in sacrificial calls to yield on some point. Or how about, "for the good of the *family*"? Have you ever invoked or received that message when it seemed necessary to give up some attitude or action that would unravel the threads of family or to take on some duty viewed as necessary for the family's unity or its reputation? In such uses, "good" finds embodiment in a particular action or response.

That understanding might seem out of sync with the commands in Amos 5:14-15 to first "seek good" and then to "*love* good" (italics added). Those imperatives make it sound as if good can be sought and loved in and of itself apart from any specific issue or need. As long as we love "good" in general, all should be well. Right?

That certainly would be the position in some forms of speculative thought. Centuries after Amos, the Greeks became especially adept at framing philosophical discourse around abstract principles. Speculative conversations about the nature of the good would be quite at home in the wisdom and wise ones of Athens, and later on in Jerusalem as Hellenism made its way into some Jewish thought in the two centuries before Jesus. I say "some" Jewish thought, because Judaism had a distinct approach to wisdom, far less interested in speculation and far more concerned with application of knowledge and insight in the practical conduct of life.

That difference can be perceived in Amos's words here. At the heart of this passage, the "good" Amos would summon us to seek and to love is not some disembodied principle. This call summons judicial decisions that protect rather than trample the poor. It calls forth judgments based on fairness and not bribes. It calls for hatred of evil and love of good to be practiced in the city gate, where justice was traditionally rendered.

The particular "good" to be sought and loved in Amos 5 may not be all-encompassing in every situation, but that was not Amos's goal. His goal was the good that took specific shape in justice.

So as we listen to this invitation to "love good," do not confuse it with a request to have a Bible study so we can all gather and discuss what the abstract principle of "good" might mean. Amos invites us to seek and love good that can never be separated from the concrete and specific circumstances of life in which good is needed. "Good" throughout the Hebrew Scriptures brings that same practical concern, one that is embedded in the fibers of creation. Recall the Genesis 1 narrative of creation. What is the recurring litany in that story, the word repeated by the Creator upon the work of almost every day? "God saw that *it* was good" (italics added), with *it* meaning what God had brought into being. In this primal story of where life in all its forms originated, "good" is located not in theoretical constructs but in the very stuff of creation. God so loved the world does not wait until John 3:16. God loved the world as good in Genesis 1.

A similar physicality of "good" comes into play in Deuteronomy. Nearly half of its twenty-plus namings of "good" refer to the good *land*. To seek and love God's good in Deuteronomy plays out in the narrative that prepares Israel for the good that is the land and for the good that is to be *done* in the land. Deuteronomy 6:18, for example, makes a causal link between Israel's occupying of the land with the injunction to "do what is right and good."

Amos invites a similar grounding of God's good. Good needs to be rooted in the relationships that form our lives and communities, our neighborhoods and national concerns. Good needs to be woven into particular words and actions that maintain genuine contact with life as it is—and need as it is known.

Amos is sorely concerned with what became of that once-promised but now possessed land of Deuteronomy, where the ethical good intended in covenant now stands in danger. Thus comes the twofold invitation of Amos 5:15: not only are we to love good, we are to "hate evil." Again, Amos has no interest in evil abstracted. Amos inveighs against specific cases of apathy and corruption that may suggest to you some modern counterparts. He points out the selling of the righteous and needy for a profit (2:6), a precursor of outsourcing jobs to sweatshops in the name of Almighty Profit and market speculations that not long ago ruined countless pensions of innocent investors while enriching a very few golden-parachuted executives. Or there is Amos's damning critique of those who are fixated only upon the "good life" they enjoy and oblivious to the needs of those around them (4:2). Likewise, his call to love and hate is not to emotional states of mind: hate and love are decisions. Hatred is rejection; in this case rejection of what Amos has catalogued in verses 10-12. Love is embrace, in this case the desired embrace of justice in the gates.

From Amos, we see that love as invitation inevitably invites a decision to act on behalf of what is good. Along with that, Amos challenges us to remember that love summons concrete and specific good to be done. In his day, that good focused upon justice in the gates. And in ours? The good we are to seek, the good we are to love, will be as varied in its forms as the needs to accomplish God's purposes for justice and mercy, compassion, and kindness, on behalf of vulnerable ones toward whom God is ever inclined to show favor. So, love good. And so, love God.

Gracious God, what is the good before me this day that you would have me love and choose? Whose is the good I might nurture, or beckon, or protect, that otherwise might fall to the side if I choose not to love? Uphold me in the good you would bring to my life, by your hand or another's, or even my own—good that draws me closer to you and deeper in love. Amen.

All right, I confess. In my adolescence (some of my "friends" would argue it lasted longer than that), I was one of those prone to falling in love with falling in love. I can remember the rush of emotion when Chris said I could walk her home from school for the first time. While it doubled the distance of my walk home, it didn't matter. I was walking on air until the oxygen departed a week or two later when another young beau caught her attention. Or the time when I mustered up the courage to phone a girl who had long been on my hope list, and lo and behold she agreed to go to the movies with me that evening. I recall, after getting off the phone, I went through my mother's copy of *The Hymnal* of the Evangelical and Reformed Church and sang lots of familiar tunes in the "Adoration and Praise" section. My ardor and love may not have immediately caught the irony of the title of that evening's movie: *Cold Turkey*.

My confession of the bedazzlements that accompany falling in love is not to ridicule such feelings or experiences. Think of the times you have fallen in love. Would you want to erase them from memory? My confession is simply offered as caution that falling in love is not the same as love. The meteoric spikes in feeling that accompany it, high and low, may mislead us into thinking love must always take form in roller-coaster runs of emotion. It will not. Love is not something we only fall into, over which we may have little or no control. Having fallen into it, love becomes ours to nurture, to choose, to remain steadfast in even when lights do not flash and feelings do not soar. Anyone can fall in love with ease and even without effort. That I know. It is not so, however, for *keeping* in love. That takes choice and work. That I continue to learn.

"Keep yourselves in the love of God" (Jude 21). Jude's sage advice takes on added weight when held in tandem and tension with the rush of falling in love. Falling in love with falling in love has a spiritual counterpart. It would be akin to the individual who immerses himself or herself in the love of one religious tradition or congregation for a short while, and then suddenly moves on to a different setting and a newfound love, and then to another, and another. Perhaps we have met such persons in our faith journey. Perhaps we have been such persons. Either way, spiritual maturity invites more than just falling in love. As Jude indicates, it means *keeping* in love.

Religious institutions may be culpable for triggering such transitory migrations. We may put out welcome mats for seekers of God. God is still speaking. Open hearts, open minds, open doors. We all have our slogans and buzzwords of hospitality. But those drawn inside by the church's rhetoric may find it hard sledding if church life is then indistinguishable from institutional bureaucracy, the morals police, or religious purveyors of partisan politics. We need to deliver on what we promise if we want people to stay.

On the other hand, those who are always on a search may be prone to the religious version of falling in love with falling in love. Momentary bursts of excitement come with each new church tried or theology explored or spiritual practice engaged. But then it begins to get old. The rush isn't there, and that is taken as evidence that the love isn't there, when in fact, it is. It is just that the faith journey is not always and everywhere about falling in love in new and different ways. It is about *keeping* in love over the long haul.

Conversion to faith, whether over the course of a lifetime starting at one's baptism as an infant, or in some singular moment of spiritual encounter and personal commitment, may be seen as our "falling" in love with God. Whether over years or in an instant, we come to see ourselves held in grace, esteem, and love that comes our way without any effort on our part. Such is the love of God into which we fall. But God, in that love, does not remove our will, or volition. Even when it comes to free and gracious love, God invites us to make that love and its keeping our own choice. Falling in love with God is an act of God's grace. *Keeping* in the love of God is a response of human will and commitment. God surely equips us in any number of ways to make that "keeping" possible. Spirit is given for the sake of our guidance. Community is offered, imperfect as it sometimes can be, to accompany us as fellow sojourners on the way. We have Scripture, we have sacraments, we have prayer and other spiritual practices to aid us.

But the choice of that love's keeping remains ours. That is why this exploration of "keeping in love" falls within this chapter's theme of love as invitation. God's love may come into our lives unannounced. We may not have recognized at the time that God's love held us, or lifted us, or nudged us. God's love may come into our lives uninvited. When we were baptized as an infant, when another showed us love when we were too angry or unforgiving to seek it, God's love came to us. But the *keeping* of that love, the keeping of that grace and mercy God casts our way, is left to us. Anyone can find themselves falling in love, including with the love of God. Jude teaches that the path of discipleship travels the way of keeping in the love of God.

How do you practice keeping *in the love of God? Make a list of those things that help you do so. Make a second list of other things that might help you keep in that love. Prayerfully commit yourself to follow at least one of those other ways during the course of this week.*

For Your Good   Deuteronomy 10:12-13

In the early 1830s, a young French lawyer toured the United States to study our penitentiary system. But apparently, Alexis de Tocqueville had his eyes and mind opened to a far larger interest. For afterward, in 1835, he published a landmark book entitled *Democracy in America*. Within that book, de Tocqueville wrote of a social ethos in America not embraced in the aristocratic and intellectual elitism dominating his native land at that time. He described this ethos as the way in which individuals in America saw their self-interest advanced by working together with others for the common good. Enlightened self-interest, if you will.

And enlightened self-interest, if you read carefully, is the motive attached to the urgings in Deuteronomy 10:12-13—including its summons to love God.

Admittedly, pairing love with enlightened self-interest may initially sound crass or even cynical. Aren't we to be selfless in our love and its consequent actions for others and for God? Yes, but remember, such high resolve is not necessarily where the spiritual journey begins for all. Additionally, selflessness and self-denial have sometimes been overmarketed to the already lowly among us, leaving the high and mighty largely high and dry from its call. The practice of love to which God calls us in Christ is not self-hatred. The practice of love emphasized by Jesus, in keeping with his Jewish tradition, is: "love your neighbor *as yourself*" (italics added). Self-hatred has no place in that command, unless you argue that hatred of neighbor is likewise acceptable in the eyes of God. Love, genuine love, invites a valuing of oneself that reflects God's valuing and loving of you. Enlightened self-interest simply puts that principle to work.

That principle comes into play in Deuteronomy 10:12. Its invitation to love is joined with four other imperatives ("fear, walk, serve, keep") issued to Israel, now poised on the edge of the Jordan prior to entering the Promised Land. The earlier chapters in Deuteronomy have already borne witness to the gracious acts of God that enact the covenant from which these commands arise. But notice, at the end of verse 13, the motive given for this response of love and all the other imperatives: "for your own well-being." Or, to be more literal, "for your own *good*" (italics added; the same Hebrew word explored in Amos two readings ago).

Do these things for your own good. In the immediate case of Deuteronomy, do these things for the good of possessing the land now before you. Do these things for the good that love and faithfulness and service bring to you and others blessed by such covenant keeping.

Do these things for your own good. In the case of our lives today, follow the lead of verse 12. Do these things for the good that comes by walking in God's ways. Such a walk joins you to God and in community with others. Do these things for the good that comes by serving God with the whole of your heart and spirit. Faith was not meant to be compartmentalized. Do these things for the good that comes by keeping the commandments of God. We live with a rich tradition in faith meant to guide our living toward God.

These invitations from verse 12 reveal that the motive of enlightened self-interest, "for your own good," does have its limits. If one's own good alone becomes the final measure for our ethics and our love, we run the risk of trying to discern in each and every action "what's in it for me." When self-interest cannot immediately be seen, then we balk or protest. I suspect the folks in the time of Deuteronomy ran up against those limits. It certainly was the case in the wilderness, when the journey became long and the grumbling started about how much better things were back in Egypt. It certainly can be the case today, when appeals to do things "for our own good" do not seem in the short-term to do us any good and may in fact feel like they are headed in quite the opposite direction.

That is why self-interest needs the qualification of "enlightened." In the case of faith covenant and community, the source of our enlightening comes in the trust that God seeks our good. For if we genuinely trust that God seeks our good with love, then it follows that our love for God will lead to our good—and in God's gracious love for the world, to the good of all.

Think back to the observations of de Tocqueville in nineteenth-century America. What he saw praiseworthy in the American spirit of that day was a willingness to link one's self-interest with working together for the common good. For in the end, all would benefit. In Christian faith, the corresponding virtue is our willingness to trust that whatever brings good to the community and to creation itself is in our best interest. The invitation to love God bids just such trust.

We do not love to force God into some transaction that gives us what we deem to be in our best interest. That would mock grace and the good God already promises. Deuteronomy invites us to love God not as some leveraged act of self-denial as in *look at me and what I'm giving up, so you better come through on your end of the bargain, God.* No, Deuteronomy invites love of God that recognizes and embraces the good such love brings to us and to all. Love God for your own good, because *God* is for your good.

Holy God, giving God, loving God: you ask no more than you already have given, and more. You invite our love of you, not to deny us life's pleasures, but that we might enjoy them in ways that are deeper, and in company that is broader, than life without love could ever imagine or hope to attain. In Jesus Christ. Amen.

Tell and Show   John 21:15-19

For many years, I was part of a writers' group that met on a monthly basis. After catching up with news in one another's lives, we each would read one or more writings and the group would engage in supportive critique. One of the frequent refrains we spoke to one another was a variation of this: "show it, don't tell it." Don't just objectively tell the reader about a character's emotion (*he was angry*) or a scene's setting (*it was autumn*). *Show* the reader the anger (*face reddened, veins in the neck jutted out*) and season (*leaves blushed with deep reds*).

Show, don't just tell.

The same is true of love and the invitation to its practice. That truth comes into play in the post-Easter scene from John's Gospel. The previous appearance of Jesus to the disciples and Thomas occurred one week after the Resurrection in the vicinity of Jerusalem. The setting of this passage is the Sea of Galilee, some sixty miles north-northeast of Jerusalem. Additional time would have passed to make the journey by foot from Jerusalem to the Sea of Galilee. So keep that passage of time in mind. It was likely well over a week since the Resurrection and even longer since Peter's threefold denial of Jesus. All this time Peter must have relived that memory over and over again in his mind and heart. Have you ever been nagged for days, or weeks, or more, by guilt? Have you ever wondered how you could let go of it?

After describing Jesus' breakfast with the disciples by the sea, the passage in John now narrates a time Jesus and Peter spent apart. In that encounter, the two engage in a liturgy, if you will, of restoration. Three times Jesus addresses Peter as "Simon son of John." The last time Jesus so addressed Peter was when they first met and Jesus named Simon as Peter (*Cephas*, Aramaic for "rock"). It was when Peter first became a follower of Jesus. The address of "Simon son of John" takes Peter back to that moment—back past the brash boastings of "I will lay down my life for you" (13:37); back past the crass threefold denials (18:17, 25-27).

Three times Jesus asks: "Do you love me?" Three times Peter answers, "You know that I love you." Thus Jesus offers a confessional opportunity for Peter to "undo" what had been avoided in the denial: for Peter to tell of his love for Jesus. But *telling* is not all that Jesus seeks of Peter's love— nor of ours. Each time Peter "tells" his love, Jesus responds with an imperative to "show" that love. "Feed my lambs . . . Tend my sheep . . . Feed my sheep." Show me. This chapter's emphasis on love as invitation finds in this scene its missional imperative: the telling of love is not sufficient for those who would follow Jesus. Love is tell *and* show.

Sometimes, the church has strayed from love's wholistic invitation to tell and show by wanting to choose one or the other. Some traditions have placed their emphasis on the "telling" of God's love. Ministries of proclamation and word-oriented evangelism are advanced above all else, underplaying or even discounting the showing of love as somehow "less important" than preaching the gospel. Worse yet, showing love through action is crudely labeled as "works righteousness." On the other hand, some traditions have gone in the opposite direction. "Showing" ministries of compassion and justice have become ends unto themselves without any accompanying word to reveal motive and grace. Whether out of embarrassment of offending others, or a deeper unease with whether we really believe what we would say, the "telling" of God's love is muted, if not silenced.

Love as invitation in John 21 does not allow the luxury of tell-only or show-only. Notice what Jesus asks Peter: "Do you love *me*?" (italics added). The question of discipleship does not begin on whether we love in generalities. The question asks the very particular and potentially scandalous: do you love *me*: the one not only risen, but crucified? The telling of God's love hinges on the particularity of that confession.

But loving Jesus does not end by *telling* love like it is. Loving Jesus invites *showing* love like it is: feeding and tending the flock, caring for the vulnerable among us. Ministries of compassion and justice and advocacy show love's way, because they show Jesus' way.

The very end of this passage from John ends with Jesus saying to Peter, "Follow me." It is not a new word for Peter. But in the restoration this passage provides, and in Jesus' invitation to love in both the telling and the showing, it is a *renewing* word that sets Peter again on love's path. So it can be with us. Love's invitation, Christ's invitation, is to tell *and* show.

NOTES

1. *The New Interpreter's Bible*, Tosefta, Sanhedrin XII 10.
2. *The New Interpreter's Bible*, vol. V, pp. 382-83.
3. *The New Interpreter's Bible*, vol. XII, p. 121.

Place yourself in this dialogue narrated by John 21. Three times Jesus asks you, not Peter, "do you love me?" Three times you answer, "Yes, Lord, you know that I love you." Three times Jesus says: "_____" What three imperatives might Jesus set before you that would invite you to show your love? To whom would such love be directed, for Jesus' sake? Write those three words down. In the course of this week, prayerfully seek ways to practice those three invitations to show love.

chapter 3

LOVE AS
LOYALTY

I n the Baseball (capital "B") of my youth, loyalty counted. True, in the days before free agency owners could be capricious in their use and abuse of players. But it was possible for teams to be known for marquee players whose names and careers were synonymous with one club. In my home of St. Louis, the Cardinals were Stan Musial and vice versa. Even for our rivals to the north, loyalty's definition forever yoked the Chicago Cubs and Ernie Banks. Rogue owners and "show me the money" agents have sapped love of the game by selling loyalty for a pottage of "what have you done for me lately?" and "who will be the highest bidder?"

Love relies on loyalty. This chapter explores how love demonstrates loyalty in a multitude of ways. We will remember God's actions in creation and redemption. We will acknowledge the call to love God with all our heart, soul, and might. We will hear Jesus name us and commission us as his beloved friends. We will explore the ways love binds us together as a community. We will examine grace that will not give up on the beloved even during times of disappointment and failure. Finally, we will acknowledge the call to grow more and more in love for one another. Love as loyalty grounds us in God's steadfast love for us and empowers us to be steadfast in love's practice.

Taking Inventory   Psalm 136

Some years back, for insurance purposes, we compiled a household inventory. It catalogued the things we owned and assessed them with an approximate replacement value. Much of that was relatively easy to do. But how do you value a collection of arrowheads gathered by your father when he was a boy? Or how do you value a small marble book sculpted by your grandfather, into which he engraved the name of his sister and her husband? Such things have no price, not because they are worthless, but because their worth resides in the stories they contribute to the narrative of where and how we have come to be.

At first sight, Psalm 136 may seem nothing like an inventory. But look more closely. The first half of every one of its verses catalogues some aspect of the story that formed Israel as a people. The broader themes reflected in these verses attest to God's actions in creation (vv. 4-9), in the Exodus and guidance through the wilderness (vv. 10-16), in the defeat of kings and inheritance of land (vv. 17-22), and a testimony to God's continuing providence (vv. 23-25). This inventory provides a summary of the core of Israel's faith. But unlike the inventories with which we might catalogue our family stories, where each piece might come to us from a different source, every single aspect of Israel's heritage and covenant in this psalm traces back to a singular origin: "for [God's] steadfast love endures forever." All that has shaped this people and covenant, and all that has shaped us as those who trace our faith back to their encounters: all comes from God's steadfast love, God's *hesed*.

The reason this psalm heads this particular chapter is simple. As noted in the lexicon provided earlier in "Using This Book," *hesed* brings to the meaning of love a strong sense of and commitment to loyalty. God's covenanting love is persistently and fiercely loyal to the life and people it brings into being. Speak this psalm's words aloud. It is not just that every verse returns to the refrain of the enduring quality of God's *hesed*. Every affirmation made in this psalm of the character of God, of the multiple works of God recited in Israel's covenant history, of the overarching and ongoing providence of God: all arise from God's steadfast, loyal, persistent love.

In the span of this brief set of verses, Psalm 136 encompasses the essence of God's activity on behalf not only of Israel but of the whole of creation. Everything, everywhere, comes to fruition because of God's *hesed*. That is the story celebrated by the psalmist in this litany of God's creative, redemptive, and providential love.

The designation of this psalm as a litany reflects a widely held view that this psalm was constructed to be a responsive song or reading in Israel's worship. But worship can suffer disconnect from the world outside of sanctuaries and carefully crafted liturgies. So what difference does it make to attribute these past actions to God's *hesed*, to love understood as loyalty, for the living of our days? In a word: remembrance. Consider the crucial importance of memory to loyalty. How can you be loyal to someone you have forgotten? How can you be loyal to an ideal or motive when you cannot remember what it meant? The exercise of loyalty requires the exercise of remembrance, in order to summon the basis for acting upon that relationship. The ability to trust in another's loyalty means a willingness to trust that he or she will remember you.

Psalm 136 remembers these great life-giving acts of God. It invites us to remember that God once acted on the basis of *hesed*. But what moves the psalm from recital of sacred history to proclamation of sacred hope is our hope and trust in *God's* remembrance of those same acts. The psalmist invokes in verse 23 God's own act of remembering as the basis of God's saving acts. The psalmist can so speak, and we can so hope, out of traditions of God's saving remembrance.

In the aftermath of the flood that devastated all of creation, Genesis 9:15 affirms that when God sees the rainbow in the clouds "I will *remember* my covenant" (italics added). God's remembrance forms creation's hope. When the people of Israel sink under the harshness of bondage in Egypt and cry out to God, Exodus 2:24 notes: "God heard their groaning, and God *remembered* his covenant" (italics added). God's remembrance begets Israel's deliverance. Psalm 136 simply builds on those traditions in verse 23: "It is [God] who remembered *us* in our low estate" (italics added). Intriguingly, that is the first time in the entire psalm that the psalmist employs the word *us*. God's remembrance moves the litany from the acts of God of old to God's acts of *hesed* today, and how it makes *us* a people and community sustained by loyal love. So give thanks to God, whose love is loyal and whose loyalty in love sustains our lives.

Try your hand at rewriting Psalm 136. Do so on the basis of your experiences of God's character and actions in your life and experience. Pair each affirmation with a refrain that, in your words, expresses what the psalmist means by "for God's steadfast love (hesed) */ endures forever." Come back to this psalm in a few days. What might you add to your litany from those days?*

Give Your All   Deuteronomy 6:4-5

My first parish was in severe northeast Washington State. I say severe, not because of weather, but because of location. We lived in the last town south of Canada and west of Idaho, one hundred miles away from the nearest metropolitan area. The relative isolation of communities in that corner of the state had the effect of making our local U.C.C. (United Church of Christ) clergy gatherings a much-valued support group. Several of us were serving our first parishes. But among us was one character, in the best sense of that word, who had years of service in ministry under his belt.

Don was a progressive among progressives and a storyteller with few peers. He told of one year's stewardship service in a church he pastored in Iowa. The custom in that farming community was to collect the yearly pledges one Sunday during the offering and count them then and there. When the pledge income came up short that day, Don instructed the ushers to pass around a new set of pledge cards. He declared they would continue doing so until the needed level of support was reached, no matter how long it took. He also told of one season in ministry when his routine consisted of heading to the airport on Monday mornings, flying to the Deep South, where he worked all week in voter registration drives of the civil rights movement in the early 1960s, then flying back on Saturday to be at church to preach the next day.

Of all the things Don ever said, though, this I remember the most. We had been talking about parish work, and some of the headaches and heartaches that come with the territory, spurring occasional thoughts of finding another career. Don's advice was: "If you think you might want to be doing something other than parish ministry, go do it. In fact, go do *anything* else. Because parish ministry is not something you can only give part of yourself to. It takes your all."

Those words can be disturbing, and not just in the context of parish ministry. The giving of one's all, no matter what the endeavor, can raise suspicions. Isn't life more about balance and moderation? Don't we get into trouble when parts of our lives become all-consuming? Isn't the demand for *all* a risk-filled request of allegiance that we can blindly pursue?

I tend to answer "yes" to those questions, but I have to admit that a powerful undercurrent of faith undergirds the counsel of my friend and mentor Don. One such undercurrent rises to the surface in the words of Deuteronomy: "You shall love the LORD your God with *all* your heart, and with *all* your soul, and with *all* your might" (italics added). The love to which Moses summoned the Israelites to aspire was to be all encompassing. Such loyalty rules out any artificial compartmentalizing of our love. Love is not limited to what we feel, or will, or yearn for, or do. Deuteronomy appeals for love that involves the whole of who we are. And just in case we might think Moses or the Deuteronomic editor overstated the case, Jesus repeats it in his teaching of the Great Commandment. In fact, Jesus raises the stakes by adding "all your mind" (Matthew 22:37) to the appeal. Love gives our all.

All leaves no wiggle room when it comes to the love we are to offer God. It is not as if we love God with our minds, until we come up against something with which we and God disagree. It is not as if we love God with our hearts, until we encounter some part of our will that we would prefer God not to bother with or alter. It is not as if we love God with our strength, until God asks us to do something within our power that we would rather not expend our energy upon. It is not as if we love God with our soul or spirit, until the growth God seeks within us comes up against some residual prejudice, or hatred of other or self, that we would insist on remaining intact. No, the love summoned by Deuteronomy beckons our all, the whole of who we are, for the sake of the whole of who we may become in God's love.

The love that commands our all is not an Old Testament word of law displaced by a New Testament word of grace. In Mark's Gospel, a young man seeks out Jesus to learn what must be done to inherit eternal life.

Jesus looks upon him with love, Mark says, and answers: "Go, sell what you own" (10:21). Luke records Jesus' words as, "Sell *all* that you own" (18:22, italics added). *All* is the gospel's call as well as Deuteronomy's, even as *all* is the gospel's love embodied in Jesus, who gives all for all.

In the end, what Don said of pastoral ministry applies to all those who would love God: our *all* is summoned. The whole of self—mind, body, spirit, strength, might—whatever comprises who we are, love seeks our all. Or, in the words of the Isaac Watts hymn: *Love so amazing, so divine, demands my soul, my life, my all.*

Make a list of ways in which love of God, and its expression in your life, comes easy to you. Make another list of ways where you struggle with what love of God seeks to ask of you. Place those lists next to one another. Are there patterns, or connections, to be seen between the two? How might loving God with your "all" impact what you have written on both lists . . . and what you have not been able to write?

Friendship   John 15:12-15

When I first came to the church mentioned in the previous reading, our conference was involved in a pilot project on Small Church Development. It studied the settings and needs of ministry in communities and congregations like the one I served. One outcome was a document listing some of its learnings. I have long since lost the list, but I did happen to write down one passage from the study:

> Churches do not necessarily want professionals, they want friends with professional skills. . . . The key to change in local congregations is the intentional development of loving relationships among staff, pastors, congregations, and their leaders.

I believe part of the reason I saved that excerpt came out of my experience at seminary, where ministry as profession—and minister as professional—had become the dominant model. Measures of readiness for ministry were much discussed and largely defined as "areas of competencies." Church calls were encouraged to resemble detailed job descriptions that would spell out what the "staff professional" was and was not responsible to do.

Good reasons exist for the professional model of ministry. It holds those in leadership accountable. It helps set clear boundaries so that power does not go abused by those in positions of authority. It has greatly advanced more equitable compensation in a vocation where there had been a long history of low salaries compared to other professions with similar training.

Even with all these good and right emphases, however, ministry as profession is still not quite the same as accounting as profession. Something more relational is at work in ministry, something that applies across the board for all who are part of Christ's community, ordained or laity. And that something hearkens to Jesus' words in John regarding friendship: "I do not call you servants any longer . . . but I have called you friends" (v. 15).

Friendship certainly ties into this chapter's theme of loyalty. How can one be a friend without loyalty? In terms of love as loyalty, recall that Jesus' naming the disciples as friends is set squarely in the midst of a passage where greatness in love goes identified as the willingness to sacrifice self for one's friends. In other words, love values loyalty to one's friends on a par with valuing one's own life. Do you have such a friend, who would move heaven and earth for your good? Would you be such a friend to another? Friendship in the terms of which Jesus speaks of it is not casual acquaintance. Friendship expresses the loyalty of love that is willing to place another before oneself.

Friendship offers a helpful image for our relationships in the community of faith, perhaps more so than that of church as family. Churches whose relationships are like family may experience difficulty in extending or allowing newcomers a place. Those on the inside of family churches often describe themselves as "close-knit." For those on the outside looking in, however, "close-knit" may be heard or experienced as "no room to squeeze through."

For such reasons, the image of friendship for understanding and practicing Christian discipleship may work better. We would do well to hear again Jesus' calling the disciples his friends. Friendship, Christ would teach us here, is more than emotional affinity to another person. It is more than having something in common so that we are friends because we both quilt or fly-fish, live on the same block, or vote for the same political party. Friendship can become the measure and means of life's greatest love, seen in the ability to set aside self for another. Our relationships to one another in the church bear with them such possibility and discipline. Christ's call to friendship carries with it a command: "You are my friends if you do what I command you" (v. 14). And that command is love.

You may have heard the old saying, "you get to choose your friends but not your family." In the context of the church, that is not entirely accurate. Jesus called his followers friends. We can therefore say that in the church, our friends have been chosen for us. As a result, there is an implicit invitation for us to demonstrate friendship toward all those who are Jesus' friends. Love as loyalty binds us to Christ, even as Christ binds us to one another by calling us friends.

Recall an act of friendship someone extended to you recently. How did it involve loyalty? In what way did it convey love? Consider someone you know, or are aware of, who stands in need of friendship. What might you do to befriend that individual in a way that expresses love? Without need of reciprocation, prayerfully and graciously extend such friendship in word or deed.

Bindings   Colossians 3:14

Rank my knowledge and experience of snow skiing somewhere south of utter novice. My one and only time on the slopes of Mount Hood left any number of indentations in the snow, many of which conformed to the shape and depth of my head and shoulders. But this much I do know: bindings are absolutely essential. Bindings attach ski boot to ski. If the bindings are too loose, you will slip out of your skis at the slightest angle or tension. If the bindings are too tight, you may well break an ankle or leg because the bindings will not release when they need to. But when bindings are right and when the skier is a skier and not a base amateur, the bindings provide the means to control what would otherwise be an out-of-control downhill plunge into a graceful experience some compare to flight. Bindings make fluid movement possible on ski slopes.

Bindings and movement: the two seem strikingly out of sync with each other. Binding is usually what we think of as restricting someone. According to some misunderstandings of the marital covenant, the *bonds* of marriage primarily tie us down or hold us back, like the overly worn joke that associates such bonds with the image of a ball and chain. How can binding, outside of this apparent exception in skiing, have anything to do with movement?

The author of Colossians implores the community to the practice of love "which *binds* everything together in perfect harmony" (italics added). The "everything" alludes to the qualities of character and relationship enumerated in previous verses: compassion, kindness, humility, meekness, patience, bearing with one another in times of complaint, forgiving one another in experiences of offense. It is quite a laundry list of virtues and practices, the individual pieces of which might seem to lead in any number of directions. But as verse 14 makes clear, the "binding" that links these qualities together and enables harmonious movement between them is love.

Why this verse, and this emphasis, in a chapter that joins love and loyalty? Binding oneself to others in community requires loyalty. It is one thing to bind oneself to another, or multiple others, when no disagreements loom and no conflicts arise and all is well. It is quite another thing to bind oneself to others when community is something other than perfect harmony. The translation of "perfect harmony" in verse 14 contains another dimension of meaning. The Greek word there is *teleiotes*. It connotes perfection, fulfillment, and maturity. The binding of love toward the goal of *maturity* rather than "perfect harmony" is a far clearer ambition and one less apt to break apart when perfection never seems to equate with experience. So "clothe yourselves with love which binds everything together with maturity" (author's paraphrase).

Love's binding toward maturity involves movement. The loyalty that binds us to others in love requires movement that allows for growth, in others and in ourselves. Maturity in faith dictates that for community to thrive, as individuals and as community we must continue to move and change in the direction God leads us. The qualities listed in those previous verses in Colossians provide signposts for ways to respond to one another in the midst of such change and growth. Love's binding connects us so that our growth will be growth together and not apart.

The previous chapter in Colossians employed the image of a human body to speak of such growth. At one point, the author wrote there of how the whole body "nourished and held together by its *ligaments* and sinews, grows with a growth that is from God" (2:19, italics added). I italicized "ligaments" for two reasons. First, ligaments are connective tissues that stretch and bend, literally making movement by bones and muscles possible. Physiological growth depends upon the ability of the body, and its individual parts, to move and flex; and ligaments help us do just that. And second, "ligaments" translates the noun form of the same Greek word rendered as "binds" in 3:14. The ligaments are to the body what love is to the community: both make possible movement that leads to growth. In the body, ligaments enable the fluid motions required for ballet and handwork and all manner of graceful action. In the church, love makes possible the fluid movement of forgiveness and compassion, forbearing and kindness, and all manner of graceful living. Love as loyalty *binds* us to one another, so that we together may move and grow toward maturity in Jesus Christ.

Blest be the ties that bind and move our hearts in Christian love.

Where could you not go were it not for Christian community? Who could you not be were it not for Christian community? Create a prayer in words, or create a prayer in art or craft, that gives thanks for the ties that bind you in faith community—and for the movement those bindings make possible in your life. Consider sharing this prayer with one with whom you share those bindings, perhaps someone who has helped you move to greater maturity of faith. With this prayer, thank them.

"How Can I Give You Up?" HOSEA 11:1-9

Just how far does loyalty go, when it does not seem to be reciprocated? How often can love be extended only to have its trust repeatedly broken? These are not idle questions. Ask parents whose child has rifled through their belongings in search of money to buy drugs. Ask a spouse whose partner has time and again been unfaithful. Ask a child whose yearning for love is met with indifference or abuse by a parent or caretaker.

The passage from Hosea engages such questions from the perspective of God's covenant relationship with Israel. The opening verses establish God's love in the imagery of birth and early childhood. Israel comes to be by God's naming, a "birthing" that results from God's calling Israel out of Egypt and into life. From there, God becomes the One to teach the toddler Ephraim (the name of the Northern Kingdom of Israel, whom Hosea addresses) to walk. God bears this child up in healing arms, and leads the people, and lifts them up with affection.

But what does such loving loyalty beget? Worship of One who delivered from Egypt is exchanged for idolatrous sacrifice to local deities. Verse 3 indicates the people are oblivious to what God has done for them. As a result, the consequences of disloyalty to God's love descend in judgment. By the end of verse 7, the people's belated calling to God does not have the effect it once did. Now there will be no raising. Tough love will be enforced. The child will have to stand on its own.

Here, you might have thought, the Book of Hosea might have ended. Disloyalty and breach of covenant has reached its logical conclusion. Except—except for a different logic at work. "How can I give you up, Ephraim? / How can I hand you over, O Israel?" (11:8).

Between verse 7 and verse 8 is a gulf that defies rational explanation. That Israel has brought down upon itself such judgment is incontestable in the Book of Hosea and other prophets. The guilt is clear.

The affront against covenant is undisputed. The disloyalty is appalling. Yet in the silence between verses 7 and 8, God *pivots*. Nothing of the previous grievances are denied or made less offensive than they were. Rather, what proves decisive is the heart and compassion of God. Even more powerfully, what proves decisive is the *identity* of God: "for I am God and no mortal" (v. 9). God cannot be held to the standard of human judgment or even human grace because God is Other than us. What that portends is not Israel's destruction but hope. God's love as loyalty goes beyond even what humans can rationally expect of loyalty. God's loyalty is utterly and entirely God's.

So what are we to make of this passage in our practice of love as loyalty? On the one hand, I am drawn back to those questions raised at the beginning about loyalty's extent and the situations that test such loyalty. I don't question those who have found through bitter experience the limits of loyalty utterly tested and broken down. Children or parents who devastate the sanity and safety of others may need to be shown the door and treated with what has popularly become known as "tough love." Human actions can be toxic to those around them in families, in communities, and in churches. When abuse of loyalty and love becomes intolerable, action is needed.

Yet I hear Hosea pushing us to another reality. Do not place the limitations of human emotion, relationship, and loyalty upon God. Sometimes we want to remake God in our own image, most often when it would be in our favor to do so. Just because we have found ourselves at the end of our patience and compassion does not mean God has as well. We may find it necessary to draw a line upon loyalty's gift when it has been abused and rejected time and time again. We may find it necessary to walk away from such a relationship. But when our loyalty reaches its breaking point, Hosea proclaims a mystery. Even in the face of the most egregious of offenses God holds on, God seeks out, God looks after, and God says, "How can I give you up?"

Using the following paraphrase from Hosea 11:1, 3-4, read through it once using your name. Listen as if God were speaking to you. What do you hear God saying to you at this moment in your life? Again, using this paraphrase, read through it once using the name of someone who tries and tests your bonds of loyalty. Listen as if God were sharing this with you as a friend. What might God be encouraging you to think, say, or do?

When _____ was a child, I loved him/her and named _____ my son/daughter.
I taught _____ to walk. I took _____ up in my arms. I led _____ with kindness and love.
I was to _____ like those who lift infants to their cheeks; I bent down and fed _____.

"More and More"   1 Thessalonians 4:9-10

One of the benefits of living in a small community was the opportunity for our son to participate in a wide variety of sports and other activities. Occasionally I helped out as a coach in the youth baseball program until the skill levels of my young charges exceeded my own. But mostly, I observed other parents, teachers, and coaches work with the youth. I saw, sometimes painfully, a variety of strategies used to motivate achievement and excellence. Appeals to school and community pride certainly ranked high, especially in athletics. Simple physical conditioning helped players move past fatigue and press on. On the downside, some motivational challenges proved counterproductive. At halftime of one game, when we struggled to make shots that normally fell in, one dour stats keeper came into the locker room and told our son and his teammates that they were stinking up the place. Perhaps this was reverse psychology intended to spark energy or emotion, but that would be giving the fellow way too much credit.

The coaches and teachers I valued most managed to build on positives in a way that motivated youth to achieve. They motivated them without browbeating and intimidation. The kids would fall over backward for these coaches and teachers, not from fear of offending them, but because they wanted to make them proud. These were the ones who, in athletics, made it possible to take on a bigger and better team and beat them because you put in more effort. These were the ones who, in education, made it possible to stretch minds and imaginations while still insisting on the basics. Don and Ryan were such coaches. Bonnie and Bruce were such teachers. It wasn't just that they encouraged the youth to work harder. They helped them *be* better.

Paul had such a purpose as he wrote to the Christian community at Thessalonica. He wanted to make an already good community even better. The opening of this Epistle made clear the fondness and regard Paul had for this community and the way they practiced their faithfulness to the gospel (1:2-7). This was a community Paul had founded. While references in the Book of Acts suggest Paul did not spend a great deal of time there, the relationships he established remained a source of thanksgiving for him. Beyond that, the Thessalonians had proved their character by their practice of love for those in their own community and throughout the region of Macedonia. But the letter was not an exercise in nostalgic reminiscing. Nor was it a call to maintain the status quo in hard times. Paul urged the Thessalonians to even greater love: "to do so more and more" (4:10).

More and more. In the mouths of some, those words might convey the message of "never satisfied." Some of those leaders of youth I alluded to in the opening were quite good at insisting on "more" from their charges. The problem was that the clamor for "more" too rarely connected to positives already achieved or to affirming and challenging growth in self-esteem. Or, worse yet, the desire for "more and more" related less to the youth's need for growth and encouragement and more to the adult's need for status and authority.

That was not the case with Paul and the Thessalonians, nor need it be the case in our journey of spiritual growth. We need not love "more and more" to satisfy some unquenchable and unattainable standard God sets for love. Paul commended the Thessalonians for the love already practiced. "More and more" was simply the invitation and encouragement to continue on that way. Love does not have a "plateau" beyond which we cannot go. Rather, love presents an ongoing discovery of its possibilities for our lives and for the lives of those around us.

To love "more and more" requires, first of all, grounding the source of our love in God's ever-flowing love for us. Our practice of love bids our loyalty to God's gracious love freely extended in our direction. Second, to love "more and more" requires "brothers and sisters." That is, we cannot love God apart from loving those created in God's image. We don't get to decide we will love God but not neighbor. If some of the harder words of Jesus are true, we don't even get to decide we will love

God but not enemy. Our practice of love bids our loyalty to God's love by graciously embracing all of humankind.

Love as loyalty has been this chapter's theme. Such love is loyal to the One whose own love is ever widening and deepening for our sake. God is loyal in love. God calls us to the same loyalty.

God, you stand by us with love loyal and persistent. You love us when our love flows in return. You love us when our love balks or withers. You are loyal in the midst of our faithfulness. You are loyal in the face of our apathy. Teach us, O God, to love with persistence and loyalty. Teach us to love you, to love one another, to love ourselves; for so you have shown us to love in Jesus Christ. Amen.

chapter 4

LOVE AS
ETHIC

Within a resource entitled *The Ordained Minister's Code,* my home denomination, the United Church of Christ, includes a statement called "The Ethics of Ministry." It outlines seven principles of conduct for what is and what is not ethical behavior for those engaged in ordained ministry. Ethics in the faith community, however, are by no means limited to clergy.

Ethics lay out acceptable, just, and needful principles of conduct for life lived in community with others. This chapter explores how various biblical traditions portray love as our fundamental ethic as individuals and as communities.

The cases made in these texts urge us to: see our indebtedness to love inseparably joining relationship to God with ethical conduct; reflect the justice God loves in the justice we seek to practice; recognize that love serves as the most revealing ethic of Christian identity; discern the motive of love that animates ethical guidelines in the Bible; recognize that lack of love betrays faith; and celebrate the psalmist's image of the "kiss of righteousness and peace" as the goal of love and ethic joined in life-giving wholeness. Love as ethic summons us to faith thoroughly rooted in holy relationship, whereby our love for God and our love for others form a seamless whole.

Indebted   ROMANS 13:8

In 1976, I moved from the Midwest, where I was born and nurtured, and landed in the Wild West. Not so wild as the warning notes sounded by some of my St. Louis born-and-bred-and-will-be-till-they-die friends as they bid goodbye, as if no wagon train would ever return to bear me or my belongings back home. But I realized after crossing the Rockies and the Selkirks that, like Dorothy in Oz, I was no longer in Kansas, or in my case, Missouri! Some things, like mile-high mountains and free-roaming elk, made that point in obvious ways. Some things less obvious, though just as real, made that point more subtly. Chief among them was a regional *esprit de corps* saturated with rugged individualism.

It's not as if other regions are devoid of this philosophy, but in the West, rugged individualism is something of a religion. Literally. Early on, I discovered one hallmark of life in my newfound Washington home: the Pacific Northwest led the nation in the highest percentage of nonchurch-goers. It still does, from what I read (see www.religionatlas.org/religion_region/COASTALNORTHWEST.htm). Various theories speculate why this is so. Some argue the pioneers and trappers and miners who first ventured out this way were averse to the trappings of civilization. Still others insist that the region's superabundance of scenic and recreational opportunities jeopardized the appeal of any institution intent on setting aside one day of the god *Weekend* for anything other than leisure and recreational good-life. A recent book, *Cascadia: The Elusive Utopia*, blends fascinating essays that examine how this haven of rugged individualism has bred its own brand(s) of noninstitutional spirituality. So what does all of this have to do with a book on love and this chapter's concern for love as ethic? Rugged individualism, in its purest form, avows a radical exaltation of self. Or, to use an older expression, it encourages one to be "beholden to no one." That is its ethic.

For a moment, Paul, writing in Romans 13:8, seems to crack the door open to such assertion of self that is beholden to no one. "Owe no one anything," he begins. Now, if taking a verse or even a phrase from a verse out of context were legitimate, you might find rugged individualists canonizing Paul as one of their patron saints. But alas, for all those who claim with William Ernest Henley in the poem "Invictus" that they are "the master of my fate" and "the captain of my soul," Paul has a bit more to say. "Owe no one anything, *except to love one another*" (italics added). In other words, we are free of all entangling alliances and involvements save one, and it happens to be the most demanding of *all* alliances and involvements. We are bound, we are indebted, to love one another. Love is the basis of our ethic.

This idea of obligation and indebtedness is not an especially appealing one, whether you live in the West or the East or any point in between. I do get the appeal of rugged individualism. It allows me the freedom to choose with whom I will be involved and from whom I will be dissociated purely at the exercise of my will. Such a philosophy plays strongly into the ease with which some move into and out of significant relationships with others. Such a philosophy plays strongly into why churches split so easily. Because when all is a matter of freedom set loose from encumbering obligations, denominational or familial or otherwise, then I owe you nothing beyond what I choose, regardless of its impact upon you. But when I owe you nothing except love, one-sided individualism finds itself yielding to two-way covenantal community.

In these days of economic duress, indebtedness as virtue and ethic may seem ludicrous. But sometimes the gospel needs to risk standing contrary to conventional wisdom for the sake of transformational faith. And in the face of ethics diluted (or is it deluded?) into thinking self-made men and women and self-enclosed communities are the pinnacle of human achievement and religious aspiration, the gospel of Romans 13:8 reminds us of our ethic as followers of Jesus. We are indebted to love one another. That debt owes to God's love for us.

To put this argument another way, imagine if God were a rugged individualist. What would the world be like? What would we be like? I would venture to say: there would be nothing, no one, save the utter silence of empty space. God would be totally self-contained and without love. Why? Love requires another for its full expression. Love does not stand alone. God has chosen the way of love, a way and a love made incarnate in Christ. We owe no one anything *but* love, because we owe God everything *for* love.

Consider a person whose love for you could never be repaid. Do two things. First, if it is possible, let that individual know the meaning of their love's gift to you. Second, focus on one individual who greatly needs a gift of love in and for their life. Owe that person nothing, except to love him or her as though Christ's love could reach through yours. For it can.

Loving What God Loves   Isaiah 61:1-3, 8

In my days of pastoral counseling with young couples preparing for marriage, I often used some form of relationship inventory. Typically the inventory consisted of several pages of multiple choice questions exploring a variety of issues: finance, interests, personality tendencies, and so forth. The couples filled out the inventories separately and returned them to me. Then we would meet to go over them after I reviewed and grouped the responses according to categories of issues. Our conversations often focused on places where interests diverged. Frequently I found myself assuring them that different interests or hobbies were not a problem and could be a strength, unless one became jealous of the other's involvements.

Looking back, one area I would do differently in such counseling would be to encourage the couple to explore more deeply a common interest they shared. I might even urge each one to make an effort to cultivate a love for what the other experienced as one of her or his passions. For in the life and nurture of relationships, loving what the other loves can become an important bond, a further opportunity to experience life's opportunities and challenges together.

I believe this encouragement to love what the other loves to be a strong dynamic in our faith journeys. To say the biblical witness and church tradition teach us to love God would not be breaking any new ground. Sometimes, however, we take the mantra of "love God" almost as much for granted as "love one another," as if saying it makes it so. It does not. Love is not fulfilled with a formula. Love's fulfillment comes in words and actions of love. So if we would love God, and if love would serve as our ethic, and if in our human relationships it behooves us to cultivate love for what the beloved loves, then what does God love? If we can discern the loves of God, we can find clues as to the sorts of actions and priorities that we can nurture and practice in our own lives. That is, we can love that which God loves.

In our passage from Isaiah 61, verse 8 makes plain what God loves: "For I the LORD love justice." You might have expected Isaiah to have said the object of God's love is worship. After all, the church spends a whole lot of time—and rightfully so—shaping and engaging in liturgy that places our relationship with God in worshipful encounter. Yet Isaiah reminded Israel and us back in 1:11-17 that worship in and of itself gives God no pleasure if it is not linked to doing good and seeking justice.

Those of us who value worship and liturgy, and count me in that camp, should perhaps seek a more objective source of what God loves than a prophet who has such suspicions of ritual. So let us turn to Israel's "hymnal" that goes by the name of the book of Psalms. What do these worship-centered creations tell us God loves? Psalm 99:4 offers this ascription of praise to God: "Mighty King, lover of *justice*, / you have established equity; / you have executed *justice*" (italics added).

What does God love and love to do? Justice. God loves to keep covenant by doing what is right, especially for vulnerable ones. God loves to get in there for oppressed and brokenhearted ones. God loves to proclaim liberty to captives and comfort mourners. God loves to bring and to *be* good news to those who haven't had good come their way in ages. At least, that's how Isaiah 61:1-3 talks about what God loves to do.

Although, to be precise about it, that's how Isaiah 61:1-3 talks about what God loves for those who love God to do. Remember, verse 1 is set in the voice of a human speaker: "The spirit of the Lord GOD is upon *me*" (italics added). Isaiah does not shift to the voice of God until verse 8 ("I the LORD love justice"). Dr. Walter Brueggemann, commenting on this passage in the Westminster Bible Companion series, notes that this chapter underscores the importance of human response to God. "The variation of speakers (human speaker—Yahweh—human speaker) indicates how intimately connected are Yahwistic resolve and human vocation."[1]

I take that to mean, in terms of this reading's theme, you cannot separate God's love of justice from our calling to love and do justice ourselves. If we truly love God, do we not want to love what God loves? And if we love God, do we not want to do what God loves to do? "For I the LORD love justice." That is our ethic, for justice is God's love.

Read the list of God-anointed actions in Isaiah 61:1-3 as a litany, with the first line of Isaiah 61:8 as the refrain ("For I the LORD love justice") spoken after each action. For example: "The spirit of the Lord GOD is upon me, because the LORD has anointed me—
FOR I THE LORD LOVE JUSTICE.
[God] has sent me to bring good news to the oppressed—
FOR I THE LORD LOVE JUSTICE."

Continue on in this manner for each line through verse 3. Afterward, select one of those lines of justice-acts that God loves. Prayerfully consider an act of justice related to it that you can and will do this week out of love for God and God's justice. Then, by the grace and for the love of God, do it!

WHAT GIVES US AWAY? JOHN 13:35

Have you ever played the game "Who Am I?" The group chooses a character for the person who is "it," ideally someone the individual would know. The game then involves that individual asking the group a series of questions about the character: what the character does, what the character is known for, where or when the character lives, and so forth. The goal is to use as few questions as possible to correctly guess the identity for "who am I." It helps to ask questions that elicit not only a range of information, but information with enough specificity to help the person who is "it" figure out the identity of the character.

Consider this variation on the game. Outsiders come to your church. They cannot ask you any question, nor can you address them. All they can do is observe what you say and do in church: in the worship service; in the council room; in situations where you and others are wrestling with a difficult issue that divides your congregation; in the fellowship group; in conversations about a personality conflict someone has with the pastor or vice versa. They can also observe what you say and do in the wider community: in your encounter with a neighbor who recently received the diagnosis of cancer, in your reaction to a stranger from a different racial background or culture, in your response to an appeal for aid to a recently unemployed worker and his family. The outsiders know nothing of you beforehand. All they know is John 13:35: "By this everyone will know that you are my disciples, if you have love for one another." Will the outsiders be able to guess that you are a disciple of Jesus from what they have seen and heard? Will they be able to see love?

At the end of the second century C.E., the author Tertullian attributes this quote to opponents of the church speaking about followers of Jesus: "See, how they love one another."[2] In spite of their rejection of the path traveled by the disciples, these outsiders gave them the begrudging due of love practiced for one another. Love gave them away as disciples.

To be sure, the church has far too often provided "See, how they love one another" with a bitterly ironic, if not sarcastic, meaning. Love was not the first thing in view while Protestants and Catholics engaged in mutual bloodletting during the religious wars around the time of the Reformation. Progress since then has sometimes merely shifted the weapons from sword and cannon to diatribe and pious posturing. "See, how they love one another" blurs when conservatives demonize all things and all ones liberal, while progressives cast conservatives as Cro-Magnon religious primitives. "See how they love one another" is eclipsed when churches fracture over the human rights of gays and lesbians. "See how they love one another" is totally out of focus when attempts to navigate the complex channels of perspectives on abortion reduce to accusations of baby-killers or woman-haters. We should not be surprised, then, when a survey released in March of 2009 (American Religious Identification Survey) shows an 11 percent drop in Americans who identified themselves as Christian between 1990 and 2008.[3] For if these are the ways we "love" one another, no wonder people decide "thanks, but no thanks."

One of the definitions of "ethics" in my office dictionary is "the rules or standards governing the conduct of the members of a . . . profession." I am sure the dictionary intends "profession" there as a vocation or occupation. The word _profession_ also means "what we profess to be true." For those of us who profess the Christian faith, the primary rule and standard governing the conduct of our members, our community, is love. Because of what we profess, because of _who_ we profess, we are bound to the ethic of love.

The church has stumbled on that ethic of its profession. But so, too, have we risen at times to the ethic of John 13:35, where love becomes what gives us away as Christ's disciples. When churches of any size lay aside preoccupation with survival for the sake of serving their communities and ministry to and with the "least of these," love gives us away as disciples of Jesus. When individuals take the time and energy to nurture children, or bring healing presence to those isolated by illness or dying, love gives us away as disciples of Jesus. When youth spend holidays rendering service on legitimate mission trips, when elders remember what it was like to be young and act with grace toward those still finding their way, love gives us away as disciples of Jesus.

Try that game of "who am I" not as a game but as a calling. Allow others to see Christ at work in you through love enacted in your life. Love is faith's best witness. Even if those whom you love do not get what you are doing, be at peace. God gets it; for God gets love.

Help me, O God, be known by my love.
Help me, O Christ, know myself loved by you.
Help me, O Spirit, know love given and love received;
both come from you, both lead toward you.

Neighborly Relations   Leviticus 19:13-18

It was said of one of the previous professors of preaching at my seminary that he was so gifted, he could take a passage out of Leviticus and make it live for the congregation. You will know what a compliment that was meant to be if you have ever waded through the chapters devoted to antiquated guidelines for animal sacrifices and ritual purifications, topics which seem distant and unrelated to the needs of people in today's congregations. But, in some places, the focus shifts from what is in order or not in regard to the community's worship to what is in order or not in regard to human conduct in a variety of settings. Leviticus 19 leans in this latter direction, where ethics comes into play. And in the text cited at the heading of this reading, the ethic of love appears.

Actually, the ethic of love comes near the end of this list of acceptable and unacceptable behavior. Like the Ten Commandments, there are more negatives ("you shall not") than positives ("you shall"). For those keeping score in this passage, the ratio is 11 to 4. Some view that in a critical way: *if religion were only more positive, telling us what to do, and not so much what we can't do, people might be more interested.* I understand these thoughts, because at times I have had them. But this ratio is instructive. Take the summary ethic of "love your neighbor as yourself." Its generality leaves the door open to a wide variety of interpretations. That is a good thing, because as an ethic it invites—it forces—us to consider all the possibilities of love's doing. Rather than catalogue a host of specific instances that might indicate *do these things and you have fulfilled love,* and thus miss out on other possibilities for the enacting of love simply because they are not listed, the ethical guideline is, *love your neighbor as yourself.* The ethic of love beckons an ongoing discernment of how that may be done in the specifics of our lives.

The list in Leviticus 19 is far more specific with what you shall not do. These are the boundaries, the limits. There is a reason why surveyors charge good money for identifying fence lines. Boundaries do little good if they are vague. The boundary lines of what is wrong and unjust like-wise need to be clear, so that intentional or accidental trespass does not occur. Some argue the later development in Judaism of growing numbers of oral traditions that became hardened into law traces to the purpose of putting a "fence" around the Torah. These efforts sought to insure that one does not accidentally trespass against the law by doing wrong.

But as for doing right, for instilling love as the ethic meant to guide our conduct toward others and even toward ourselves: do we need to set boundary lines for these things as well? Paul addressed this issue in Galatians in a matter including, but not limited, to love. "The fruit of the Spirit is love, joy, peace, patience, kindness, generosity, faith-fulness, gentleness, and self-control. There is no *law* against such things" (Galatians 5:22-23, italics added). Love—and each of these other qualities—needs no boundary lines to put a limit on its expres-sion. For once we set boundary lines and limits, we risk leaving the im-pression that love is exhausted by the one thing that is declared, or specified, and we need go no further.

Does this mean we can and should always leave the command and ethic of love vague and unspecific? No. Vague love is an oxymoron. For love to be love, it has to be specific. But whenever the church ventures into the realm of specifying what love invites or summons, there always needs to be a caveat of "but there is more to it than that." Sometimes the church has settled for interpreting the specifics of love too narrowly, par-ticularly when it comes to institutional well-being. We have at times made it seem as if love for one another was pretty much limited to those within the ranks of Christian community. When it came to Jewish or Muslim brothers or sisters—well, *brothers or sisters* was not used. At other times the defining lines have become even narrower, as in love one another who think and believe and vote as we do; but as for those who don't, es-pecially those who oppose us, they are outside the pale. In such times, the words of Jesus come in haunting ways upon us: "If you love those who love you, what credit is that to you?" (Luke 6:32). Love is not defined by its limits but by its expansion.

Love is our ethic. It is not an ethic to be gleaned from meticulous lists of what constitutes love in days gone by. Love is an ethic to be discerned in the present opportunities to seek what is good and just toward those who are family or neighbor or stranger, or, if we really go out on a limb and take Jesus at his word, enemies (Matthew 5:44).

"You shall love your neighbor as yourself." Don't just take that on the word of Leviticus. Take that on the word of the One Leviticus cites in that very verse: "I am the LORD."

Repeat the words of Leviticus aloud: "You shall love your neighbor as yourself." Consider someone who is your neighbor, that is, someone whose need or situation has become known to you. Prayerfully reflect on what the ethic of love calls you to do (and not do) on that person's behalf and for that person's good. Heed all the "not do's" and pick out one positive action that would evidence love. Do it this week, not because you must, but because you may.

Integrity   1 John 4:20-21

The vice-presidential debate of 1988 pitted Republican candidate Senator Dan Quayle against Democratic candidate Senator Lloyd Bentsen. During the debate, Quayle sought to underscore his qualifications for the office, in light of the much longer tenure in the Senate of Bentsen by comparing his own time of service in the Senate to that of the late President John F. Kennedy. Senator Bentsen responded with one of the most memorable rebuttals in any political debate: "Senator, I served with Jack Kennedy, I knew Jack Kennedy, Jack Kennedy was a friend of mine. Senator, you're no Jack Kennedy."[4]

The church addressed by the First Epistle of John had suffered a significant schism in its life. A group had separated itself from the community. They apparently questioned the faith of those left behind and promoted themselves as the true Christians. It is even suggested, reading between the lines of 1 John 1:8, that they considered themselves without sin. Much of the tone of the First John (as well as Second and Third John) reassures the members of the community discarded by the "true" believers. The overarching call to love aims to provide the community with the means to hold together through this difficult time.

Dwelling on the theme of love in First John, however, does not mean the Epistle is everywhere and toward everyone conciliatory. The claims made by the separatists are held up against the evidence of their lives and actions. They, too, apparently talk the talk of love. They, too, apparently promote themselves in the language of Jesus' command to love one another. But like Bentsen to Quayle, the author of First John fashions a rebuttal that grows out of the opponents' alleged claims: "Those who say, 'I love God,' and hate their brothers or sisters, are liars; for those who do not love a brother or sister whom they have seen, cannot love God whom they have not seen" (4:20). Those are harsh words. Those are line-in-the-sand words. Yet they are true words: true to the ethic of love.

The ethic of love confirmed in this rebuttal has primarily to do with the matter of integrity in our lives. "Do as I say and not as I do" is lousy parenting, and it is worse theology. In the particular case of the early Christian community addressed by the Johannine Epistles, loving God and loving one another are not two independent actions from which we can choose one and ignore or contradict the other.

The force of that point is made by the author's depiction of those who mingle love and hate as "liars." In the language employed in the writings attributed to John, *liar* is not simply a term for being ethically challenged. John 8:44 identifies the devil as "the father of lies." Elsewhere in this Epistle, lies are associated with those who assert knowledge of God without obedience of God (2:4) and those who deny Jesus as the Christ or Messiah (2:22). Hating the brothers and sisters is not merely unsociable. It makes us liars and separates us from God.

The harshness of the Epistle's tone here might strike us as over-the-top and perhaps verging on showing the same disregard or hatred that the letter condemns. Care does need to be taken in such matters, lest we adopt the divisiveness and hatefulness we find repugnant in others. But we are also commended elsewhere to speak truth to power—especially when power would abuse the language of love with the exercise of hatred. The ethic of love at work in Jesus' life and ministry led him to words and acts of great compassion many times—and at other times to words and acts of harsh confrontation. Mark 3:4 notes Jesus' anger at some who watched to see if Jesus' healing of another would give them opportunity to accuse. Jesus accused some religious leaders of hypocrisy for their obsession with minor observances and for their neglect of justice and love (Luke 11:42). Jesus resorted to physical violence by overturning the tables of moneychangers, even making a whip of cords to assist in the action (John 2:15).

The biblical ethic of love is not synonymous with *going along to get along*. The ethic of love is not always and everywhere a smiling face and an acquiescing spirit. The ethic of love demands integrity: between love of God and love of one another, between principles of faith and practices of daily living. The ethic of love does not put up with anything in the name of love. Rather, the ethic of love calls us to gauge and measure the whole of our lives by its good.

Love of God and hatred of others makes liars of any who would profess love's ethic. Love's ethic demands love of God giving rise to love of others.

Prayerfully, and honestly, consider the hatreds with which you wrestle. For the moment, do not dwell on how they came to be. Rather, focus upon what those hatreds make of you. Reread 1 John 4:20. In the light of those words, again consider what those hatreds make of you. Read 4:21. Ask: what would God make of you? Seek God's help in prayer, and as needed in counsel with a trusted guide, in moving past those hatreds.

THE Kiss of Love: Righteousness and Peace   Psalm 85:7-13

"Kisses" are not frequent in the biblical narrative. When they do appear, they often accompany critical moments. When Esau finally meets up with the brother who stole birthright and blessing from him, his gracious choice of reconciliation is embodied by his kiss of Jacob (Genesis 33:4). Jesus tells the parable of a loving father who, upon sight of a son whose earlier request for his share of the inheritance intimated an attitude that the father had not died soon enough, receives the errant child with a welcoming embrace and kiss (Luke 15:20). The kiss of Jesus by Judas only heightens the stark nature of betrayal (Luke 22:47-48). So what meaning does Psalm 85:10 intend to convey when it declares: "righteousness and peace will *kiss* each other" (italics added)?

Take a look at the verb tenses beginning in verse 8 and running through the end of the psalm at verse 13. With one exception, everything is future tense ("will speak . . . will meet . . . will kiss . . ."). The overall passage frames the hope of its readers. But rather than "spiritualize" hope, as Walter Brueggemann notes in his comments on this passage, the psalm anchors hope in the practical matters of justice.[5] "Righteousness" appears three times in verses 10-13 and the land's fertility in verse 12.

So, if such fulfillment of hope is to come, and if love's ethic is to be embodied in daily life and community, what needs to happen? In the imagery of the psalmist, a kiss is in order: the kiss of righteousness and peace. A kiss that seals the relationship between these two, a kiss that reveals the affection and respect that righteousness and peace have for and need from each other.

Let us also keep in mind that a kiss can be an expression of longing. A kiss can signify the feeling of two who do not find themselves whole in some ways without the other, without the beloved. A kiss culminates services of marriage or commitment. It is the final symbolic seal of vows made and lives joined. Justice and peace may be seen to have such a relationship. Can there be genuine justice when God's shalom is absent?

Warrings or fears keep us unsettled, making justice a secondary concern to survival. Can there be genuine peace when God's justice is absent? Inequities and unfairness keep us on edge and lead to resentments or envies that lead to violence and the disruption of peace. The psalmist brings the imagery of a *kiss* between righteousness and peace out of such longing for the two to finally be fully united. Neither can be whole without the other. Without such wholeness of justice and peace, hope dissolves into wishful thinking of things that never will be and thus cannot be trusted.

So how, or why, does this particular *kiss* relate to this chapter's emphasis on love as ethic? The verse that ends with the kiss of righteousness and peace begins with "steadfast love and faithfulness will meet." Love (the Hebrew word *hesed*) and faithfulness go hand in hand, as do justice and peace. Love's ethic, love's way of ordering life and community, is all about this earnest longing and final sealing of commitment expressed in the metaphor of a kiss.

In the psalm, such longing and commitment is attributed to a personified righteousness and peace. But remember, the psalm is not written as an abstract thesis. It is an evocation of faith and hope on the part of its audience, Israel—and through Israel, on our part. The longing for and commitment to justice and peace finally and fully united is an invitation to community. It is a call not only to make such desire and intent our attitude but to translate that into concrete acts that do justice and make for peace in these days and in these places where we live.

"Righteousness and peace will kiss each other." Those last two words are also important for those who would practice the ethic of love. "Each other" suggests the complementary nature of this call. It is not that some of us get confined to do the justice part; others get relegated to the peace part; and every once in a while we check in to see where the other is, just in case we are working at cross purposes. The inseparability of justice and peace makes it critical to practice these qualities and hopes of God's realm together, as one piece.

The psalm longs for the joining of justice and peace, as does the ethic of love to which they both belong. Christian hope and Christian love fill us with both longing and commitment to see God's good come to us and to all creation. Until then, the ethic of love seeks to channel that desire into our participation in the ways and works of God's justice and peace.

NOTES

1. Walter Brueggemann, *Isaiah* (Louisville: Westminster John Knox Press, 1998), 212.

2. Tertullian, *Apology*, ch. 39, 7.

3. See www.americanreligionsurvey-avis.org/reports/highlights.html.

4. See www.debates.org/index.php?page=october-5-1988-debate-tran scripts.

5. Walter Brueggemann, *Theology of the Old Testament* (Minneapolis: Fortress Press, 1997), 482.

What longings does faith stir most in you: in regard to justice; in regard to peace? Identify an action you can take that would give expression to that longing, and give witness and/or embodiment to that justice and peace. Pray about it. Consider talking to someone who might share a similar longing. Then, alone or with another (or others), carry out that action. As you do so, entrust this act into God's hands and purposes, that good will come of it and that love will be shown.

chapter 5

LOVE AS COMPASSION

*C*ompassion has roots that mean to suffer with or for another. In common usage, *compassion* connotes a willingness to share another's trying experiences, and in the sharing, to do something in response. Compassion makes allowance for the needs of others to sometimes interrupt our personal agendas. In the final word, compassion is an expression of love. To know ourselves loved by God is not just to make us feel warm inside. Such knowledge awakens words and actions of compassion on behalf of others.

The passages and readings in this chapter beckon us to move deeper into the nature and practice of compassion. We will explore it as a learned behavior, with God as our mentor. We will look at it as a form of holy entertainment, whereby strangers can be greeted with hospitality rather than hostility. We will see it as the willingness to risk loving another, even when that love might jeopardize us. We will understand that it calls us to have the same mind and to practice the same compassion as Christ. Finally, we will discover that compassion dares us to embrace those who are often not embraced by society or by the church. Love as compassion bids us enter into community with all who are sisters and brothers of Christ and to realize how wide a circle of love that truly is.

LEARNEd BEHAViOR   DEUTERONOMY 10:17-19

Mentors and mentoring have come to prominence over the past decade or so. In the business world, up-and-coming executives are advised to find experienced colleagues in their field who can counsel, advise, and model what their professions require. In work with at-risk youth, mentoring programs provide guidance and support from trusted adults and peers. In the church, several confirmation curricula go beyond religious instruction to intentionally pair youth with adults in the congregation who help model the Christian faith into which they are being nurtured. The essence of mentoring can be discerned in the very origin of the word. In his book *The Odyssey*, Homer describes how the hero Ulysses selected a trusted friend to provide guidance and direction to his young son Telemachus while Ulysses set out on his journey. The name of this friend to whom Ulysses entrusted his own child's growth and development? Mentor.

The value of mentors and mentoring traces to a fundamental truth of human growth and development: behavior is learned. The old adage about "do as I say and not as I do," while clever, is an invitation to failure. For better or worse, as children and youth, we learn more from what we see adults in authority do in and with their lives. Far too often the heartbreaking consequence in children of adults who are abusive, whether of alcohol or by violence, is that they in turn become abusive. These children see the destruction wrought in that behavior. They hear the lectures about not going down that road. They may even be able to verbalize that warning themselves. Frequently though, the behavior they observe and experience becomes the behavior they adopt. Learned behavior also has possibilities for cultivating good within and across generations. How do we learn love embodied in the practice of compassion? Where and in whom do we find a mentor to learn such behavior?

Deuteronomy 10:17-19 begins with praise of God and a recital of qualities integral to God's character. Impartial. Takes no bribes. Executes justice. Loves the stranger. This passage does more here than give a character study of Yahweh to educate us on the abstract nature of Deity. More practically, Deuteronomy lays the groundwork for its "hook" of learned behavior: "You shall also love the stranger, for you were strangers in the land of Egypt" (v. 19). In other words, the call for us to love stems from God's own exercise of compassionate love toward strangers and sojourners. Israel has been *mentored* in compassionate love by God's own love for them while they were strangers in Egypt. God "mentors" compassionate love through modeling impartiality and fairness, by executing justice, and by providing food and clothing. So returning to questions of how we learn compassionate love and where we find a mentor of such behavior, the answer in Deuteronomy is "God." We learn of love and compassion in the character and action of the God who loves strangers as well as the people of Israel.

The link between love of stranger and love as compassion derives from the meaning of this word translated as "stranger." The Hebrew word is *ger*. In some places it is rendered as "sojourner." *Sojourner* evokes the image of journey, which has many positive connotations. But *ger* in its original meaning is far more of an at-risk refugee than a happy wayfarer. *Ger* was someone without land, and as such was routinely without protections to shelter him or her from abuse by the landed and powerful. So think of *ger* more as refugee, or even illegal alien: someone passing through, who might be seen as a threat. *Ger* was precisely the condition of Israel in Egypt, at the mercy of unmerciful and uncompassionate authorities.

God mentors love for the *stranger* and in doing so, evokes the empathy and compassion that come by recognition that God so loved us. Love as compassion is thus learned behavior from God. Love as compassion is not God telling us to do what God will not. Love as compassion is God demonstrating for us what God has already done toward the stranger, toward the vulnerable, toward you and me. God mentors us in compassionate love.

Who might we mentor with compassionate love in order that they might experience and learn of God's love, then go and do likewise?

Who have been the mentors in your life? For your vocation? Your ideals? For the practices of family and friendship? For your growth in faith? How has God been a mentor to you? Where do you most see or need God's mentoring at this point and time in your life? What behavior can you learn from God?

ENTERTAINMENT   HEBREWS 13:1-2

What's a word like *entertainment* doing in a chapter on love as compassion? Consider these three words in Hebrews 13:1-2: mutual love,
hospitality to strangers, and entertain. In English, it might be hard to see
the connections between the three. In Greek, however, the links are
more visible: *philadelphia*, *philoxenia*, and *xenizo*.

The meaning of *philadelphia* may be familiar to us from the motto of
Pennsylvania's "city of brotherly love." Love of brother and sister: that
link with love as compassion makes obvious sense. Familial love forms
one basis for how we are to love one another in compassionate ways. The
call to love those to whom we are related by reason of kinship or friendship or community affiliation does not surprise. Loving those who love
us, loving those we know and who know us, has a certain reciprocity that
the translation of *philadelphia* as "mutual love" undergirds.

But *philadelphia*, mutual love, shares the same prefix with a word in
verse 2 that points to quite a different direction for our love. The translation of this word as "show hospitality to strangers" does not quite catch
the challenge of the Greek *philoxenia*: literally, "love of stranger." This
directive provides an unsettling alternative to what modern culture cul-
tivates in "stranger danger," an attitude that risks casting all persons different from us in a negative light. And it is not Hebrews 12 alone that
promotes the imperative to love the stranger among us. Both Romans
12:13 and 1 Peter 4:9 employ this same word to address their communities with a call to love that is as compassionate to those outside the circle as to those within.

But why use the word *entertainment* as this reading's title? Verse 2
follows the call to *love the stranger* with the reminder that, by doing so,
"some have *entertained* angels without knowing it" (italics added).
Entertain translates *xenizo*, part of the same word family as *xenos*
("stranger") and *philoxenia* ("hospitality"). Biblically speaking, the
origin of entertainment is not a song-and-dance show. The origin of

entertainment is not even inviting friends over for dinner and conversation. The origin of entertainment is welcoming strangers with hospitality. Or, to set this in the framework of this chapter's theme: to entertain is to practice loving compassion toward outsiders as well as insiders. The mutuality of love in verse 1 and the inclusivity of love in verse 2 complement each other. For in the balance of love between known ones and new ones comes the grace of acting with compassion toward both, knowing both to be loved and welcomed by God.

This "informational" content regarding Greek word studies strengthens the case for the "formational" thrust of this passage upon the *practice* of love-driven spirituality. Love as compassion and love of the stranger is more than politeness; it is a biblical mandate. As individuals and as communities, we need to hear again the distinction made here about what truly constitutes entertainment. It is not the self-serving distraction from the world around us to which it has often been reduced. To entertain, in the language and spirituality of Hebrews, is to welcome strangers. It is to make our lives and churches open to those in need of a place to find themselves in the presence and providence of God.

To exercise mutual love does not constitute an excuse to love those we like and who are like us and leave it at that. To exercise mutual love opens a wider vision of God's call to exercise compassion to those inside and outside our usual boundaries and comfort zones of community. We are invited to offer such welcome not as an imposed duty but as a gracious opportunity. Hebrews 12:2 describes the opportunity afforded by extending hospitality toward strangers as bearing the potential for entertaining angels "without knowing it."

And not only angels, if another New Testament witness may be added. In Matthew's Gospel, the word *stranger* occurs five times. Four of those times come in Jesus' parable of the Last Judgment (25:31-46). Each time it is in reference to an act or to a missed opportunity of welcoming a stranger. Except, the stranger is, in truth, no stranger at all. For in Jesus' words recorded by Matthew: "I was a stranger and you welcomed me" (v. 35). The welcoming of strangers with hospitality, in Gospel terms, becomes the welcoming of Christ. Now that's entertainment!

Consider an individual, a family, or a group in your wider community who may need your hospitality. What is the hospitality they need? Might you invite them to join you at a meal or at church? How might you "entertain" them in the sense reflected in the reading above? Pray for God to lead you as an instrument of welcome and hospitality, either alone or with others. Offer hospitality in the name of Christ.

To Love Another as Self　　　　1 Samuel 18:1-3; 20:12-17

No small irony exists in reading the story of Jonathan and David in these polarized times in the church. Even the hint of love between two persons of the same gender can draw lines (more accurately, dig trenches) or generate worried *we don't talk about such things here* advice for maintaining uneasy truces in pews or ordination committees. Part of the problem is our culture's tendency to sexualize any expression of love that makes us nervous. We are OK with love when we confine it to aphorisms of "love your neighbor" or "God is love." But when love comes in the context of relationships that make us uneasy, or are apt to be taken out of context, we get worried that sex is going to be involved.

If you think I am being too harsh here, consider this scenario. The preacher at your church posts the following sermon title, based on this passage, on your church bulletin board, the Saturday religious section in the newspaper, and your website: "Men in Love!" What will be the reaction in your community, in your church, in your home? Will you think the risk taken by such a provocative title, presumably to drum up attention, will be worth the reaction?

Perhaps it seems we are getting far afield from the text itself and the promoted theme of "to love another as self." Actually, we are getting at its core: namely, the risk that comes with love so compassionate that it expresses love for another as equal with love for one's very own self. That is exactly how Jonathan confesses his devotion to David, not once but twice: "he loved him as his own soul" (Samuel 18:1, 3). That such love was reciprocal, though still fraught with danger, comes in the oath David swears to Jonathan upon his love for him: "for he loved him as he loved his own life" (20:17). Such intensity of love is risky, not only emotionally, but in this case politically. The king's son avows a love for another besides the king—and Saul is quick to respond to Jonathan's feelings for David: "Do I not know that you have chosen the son of Jesse to your own shame, and to the shame of your mother's nakedness?"

(20:30b). One clear risk of love as between Jonathan and David is misunderstanding. Saul misunderstands that love as rejection of a son's love for his father, not to mention a king-in-waiting's love for the one still king. Love rejected can become bitter and caustic, as Saul's response to Jonathan makes clear.

But love as compassion is willing to take that risk. That is the essence of compassion: to be motivated, to be devoted, to seek the other's good, come what may. Jonathan's expression of love for David in Chapter 20 comes in the middle of a narrative wherein Jonathan risks censure by his father for the sole purpose of determining whether it is safe for David to return to court. Jonathan is utterly loyal to David, a point made clear in verses 14-15 by Jonathan's appeal to "faithful love." The Hebrew word is one we have encountered a number of times in this book: *hesed*. Steadfast love. Loyalty above and beyond the call of duty. It is only natural that compassion and *hesed* should be so joined. For what makes it possible to be compassionate to another, even when such compassion puts self at risk, if not a compelling sense of loyalty to the other bound in love? Jonathan so loves David, with a love that risks even self for the good of the beloved.

Who are the ones, or perhaps the one, whom you love as you love your very self? Who are the ones who love you as they love their own selves? Please know, at this moment, even if you can think of no one, you are so loved by God. That is, after all, the essence of the story of Jesus. In Christ, we are loved by One who loves us as Christ's own self. If that were not the case, why bother plodding along three or more years with disciples who had a habit of not getting things on the first take, or the second take, or more? If that were not the case, why risk the indignities heaped upon him in Jerusalem, and ultimately the cross?

But that was the case. *Love* was the case: love for you, love for me, love for the ones we like and get along with, love for the ones who rattle our cages, love for the ones we hate. We catch glimpses of such love in the love Jonathan had for David. We catch glimpses of such love when we find ourselves somehow, some way, seeking another's good even when it comes with risk to our reputation or well-being. We catch glimpses of such love when another will not give up on us, will not let go of us, for no other reason than that they love us as much as they love themselves.

To love another as one's own self is the story of love as compassion lived by Jonathan for David. To love another as one's own self is the story of love as compassion incarnate by God for the whole of creation. To love another as one's own self can be the story of love as compassion played out in your life. Who will you love as your own self?

Love me into the ways of love, O God. May the compassion you pour out upon me take shape in the compassion I offer to others. May the risk you have taken with me be answered in the risk I take in compassion's gift to others. Anchor me in your steadfast love. In Jesus Christ. Amen.

Christ-Minded   Philippians 2:1-5

During my last full-time pastorate, St. John's Hospital in Longview, Washington, annually observed a Pastoral Care Week. Area clergy were invited for a luncheon and program arranged by the chaplains. One year's program that I attended focused on organ donation. Speakers from various agencies, along with three recipients of organ donations, offered a very compelling and moving presentation. At that time, corneal transplants represented the most remarkable age range. The youngest recipient to date had been a 34-day-old infant, while the oldest was 102 years old. In both cases, the gift of sight resulted.

Organ transplants have become a fascinating component of modern medical technology, even as their cost has created one of health care's most controversial debates. Hearts, kidneys, corneas, livers, skin, bone, and cartilage can be given to extend and enrich life. The limitation of many of these transplants is that the donor must be deceased. Decisions have to be made quickly, conditions have to be right, for transplants to be possible. Contrary to several generations of Frankenstein movies, medicine has yet to successfully transplant the human brain. I am not aware of anyone or any group seriously working on the mechanics of such a transplant. Too much still needs to be learned about the brain's mysteries. Yet what does Paul write in Philippians? "Make my joy complete: be of the same mind, having the same love. . . . Let the same mind be in you that was in Christ Jesus" (Philippians 2:2a, 5).

The connection between unity of mind and unity of love becomes even more intriguing when we consider the close of verse 1 that leads into this call of shared minds: "If then there is . . . any compassion and sympathy" (2:1). Having the mind of Christ of necessity involves compassion. The word Paul uses here, translated as "compassion," also has a peculiar link to the opening paragraphs' theme of physical organs. The Greek word translated as *compassion* literally refers to the intestines, viewed in the ancient world as the seat of emotions. Perhaps the closest contemporary parallel would be to "gut" feelings, those stirrings that go beyond our rational thought processes and take us into the realm of intuition and "deep down" feelings.

Love as compassion is not a rational-as-in-academic ideal. Love as compassion pulls the mind into the current of feelings for another that cannot be ignored and must be acted upon. To speak of compassion that moves us toward others in tandem with having the mind of Christ is not simply Paul's argument. It is also Jesus' lived example. The mind of Christ is not merely what Jesus *thinks* about things. Because of compassion, the mind of Christ is what Jesus *does* about things. In Matthew 14:14, compassion moves Jesus to heal the sick, and later in 15:32 compassion results in the feeding of four thousand. In Luke 7:13-15, compassion moves Jesus to raise the dead son of the widow of Nain. To share the mind of Christ is to risk feeling another's pain or need, so that love as compassion may be set loose to drive actions of ministry.

"Be of the same mind, having the same love" (Philippians 2:2). Sometimes, I fear, we miss the point of this verse by presuming the first half means we all have to think alike. And if I catch you thinking a different way about God or Jesus, or thinking a different way about abortion or war or gay rights, then you must not be a Christian. Being Christ-minded is not a summons to lock-step thinking. It is an invitation into community that is grounded in compassionate love.

Consider the qualities evoked in verse 1, and then in the hymn-like litany beginning at verse 6. Christ-mindedness is an invitation to generosity of spirit and humility in service. Christ-mindedness is an incitement to love with compassion. Think back on what compassion led Christ to do. Heal. Feed. Raise. In Luke's parable of the loving father, compassion sets that parent running to embrace the prodigal son before he could utter any word of confession or remorse. The loving father in the parable demonstrates what it means to be Christ-minded through his actions of compassion, love, and grace. Be of the same mind. Have the same love. Exercise the compassion of Christ.

In prayer, ask Christ: "Who is on your mind right now?" Imagine the faces, and situations, that come to your mind as you ask that question and listen in silence. In prayer, ask Christ: "Who among them would you have to be on my mind, and why?" Observe a time of quiet. In prayer, ask Christ: "How might I share your mind, by sharing your compassion toward them?" Write in a journal what comes to mind, and heart, and gut. Act on that call to compassion.

EXTREME COMPASSION   MATTHEW 5:43-48

I have always considered myself something of a sports fan. I grew up in St. Louis in the days when mayors were mere figureheads while Stan Musial and then Bob Gibson reigned over the city. Being a sports fan was a civic duty. That day's trinity of baseball, football, and hockey was secure in its orthodoxy. In these latter days, however, new sports have emerged, many of them dubbing themselves as "extreme." I'm not sure how that name evolved, or why previous sports like mountain climbing or running a wisp of a flanker on a crossing pattern over the middle with Dick Butkus waiting were not considered to be extreme. Times change. Sports change. But some things stay the same. Extreme sports provide athletes with a showcase. Like other popular sports in days when I was growing up, promoters seek to cash in on the interest.

Extreme sports, extreme *anything*, might seem to be a curious entry into matters of faith and spiritual formation. We in the church prefer things to be more moderate. We have our suspicions about those who get carried away with things. Too much social action, too much Bible thumping, too much of most anything, really. The fear is if we get too far out on the edge, we will lose our balance and fall out of mainstream beliefs and the communities that value them. There certainly are reasons to seek balance and equilibrium in our life and in our churches. Then again, there certainly are biblical texts that aim us in the opposite direction— in the direction and practice of the extreme.

Consider the counsels in Matthew 5:38-46. "Do not resist an evildoer . . . turn the other [cheek] . . . love your enemies and pray for those who persecute you." Ouch. That sounds extreme—or, more scandalously, *Jesus* sounds extreme. Then again, such love and compassion that seeks the good of the very ones who seek no such good for us *is* extreme. It challenges long-held assumptions ("an eye for an eye . . . hate your enemy") with a radical understanding of what it truly means to be children of God (v. 45).

Where do we see such extreme compassion actually put into practice? In parable form, we have the embrace of the prodigal by the father. In the Crucifixion, we have Jesus asking God to forgive his crucifiers. Some might argue that such stories were well and good for their day, but that these days are different. We are not Jesus and thus cannot hope—and probably should not even try—to risk such extreme compassion, lest it be misunderstood.

My wife is a 911 dispatcher. I remember when Judy called me early one September morning from work and told me to turn on the TV—which I did, just in time to see the second airliner crash into the World Trade Center. She and her coworkers, though removed by a continent from those events, were agonized by what their dispatcher cohorts in New York endured when the radio transmissions of firefighters and police inside the Trade Center fell deadly silent. I also remember when she came home from work later that week. Judy said one of her coworkers, a mother of two teenagers, had gone home on September 11 fully expecting a conversation with the girls about what had happened. She was right, though the talk took a totally unexpected turn. One of her girls confided that she was thinking about the hijackers who had committed this horrific act. She imagined how surprised and saddened they must have been to enter into God's presence, along with the victims of their act, realizing only then what they had truly done. I would be ashamed to tell you my thoughts toward the hijackers in that time. In stark contrast, here was a young girl, in the age demographic of those most drawn to extreme sports, uttering what was probably one of the few Jesus-like expressions of extreme compassion toward the hijackers.

I've heard "love your enemies" all my life, but I heard it again in that girl's ability to feel something other than hate toward the easily and most justifiably hated. Extreme, I'd say, but I suspect her insight is Jesus' point. "Love your enemies" is not supposed to be an axiom that would look good in needlepoint over the mantle. "Love your enemies" is a disconcerting charge to exercise compassion toward the very ones from whom we would prefer to withhold compassion. Extreme compassion, loving the unlovable, goes to the heart of what Jesus seeks and what Jesus lives.

> *Read aloud, "Love your enemies and pray for those who persecute you." Read it again—only now, imagine the voice to be that of Jesus. He is speaking directly and only to you. Write a journal entry, or do a piece of artwork, that reflects on what those words say to you. Who comes to mind as someone who could receive such extreme compassion? As you do this activity, be open to ways you can put these words into practice. Prayerfully seek God's presence, Christ's compassion, and the Holy Spirit's power to make that step as you are able and as you are ready.*

Compassion as the Final Word   Isaiah 54:7-10

If you have not encountered the poet Ann Weems, I encourage you to do so. Her book *Psalms of Lament* evidences extraordinary faith and spiritual depth. The impetus of that work owes to a singular event in her life. Her son had been murdered less than an hour after his twenty-first birthday.[1] Some might never move beyond the despair imposed by such a tragedy. Some might seek to deny it in a triumphalistic piety that claims God intended the tragedy for some greater good. Ann Weems chose a third way, a way that reflected on the God-forsakenness of her loss with the resources of her faith and the biblical tradition of lament. It is a way that does not let God off the hook in the midst of such an event, yet it is a way that does not let go of God either.

Isaiah 54:7-10 poses a similar movement. The Scripture contains words and assurances of love and compassion and peace, but it begins with the acknowledgment of abandonment—and not abandonment of God by Israel. Quite the contrary: "For a brief moment / I abandoned you. . . . In overflowing wrath for a moment I hid my face from you." The "I" in those verses is God, the "you" is Israel in exile. These are remarkable words in Scripture, for they confess when God abandoned Israel.

As if to mollify that extraordinary admission, the text twice notes that it was but for a moment, as if shortness of duration made it all right. But do you recall the movement of time in the midst of a situation of extreme duress in your life? I remember when I worked as a volunteer for our local ambulance crew and my initial experience of being first on-scene at a cardiac arrest. I had to begin CPR alone. Eventually, interminably I thought, others arrived to help and then take my place. I asked the ambulance director afterward why it took so long, as it seemed to me I was there by myself ten minutes or more. She smiled, out of experience, and said it was only three or four minutes. The meaning of "a brief moment" depends entirely upon our point of view. Israel's "brief moment" of exile had been over fifty years. What does "brief moment" mean when the experience of abandonment comes in the death of a child or spouse, the loss of a job, of a home, or of retirement investments in an economic downturn? Moments can seem to last a lifetime.

In Isaiah 54:7-10, there is a disarming frankness to the testimony of God's abandonment. Not even the suggestion of its "brief moment" can erase the candor, especially when that moment for Israel stretched over generations. But abandonment is not the final word of this passage. The word that theologically and literally frames this passage at beginning and ending is: *compassion*. Abandonment, however brief or long its duration, will yield to God's compassion. In the context of Isaiah, compassion takes form in God's gathering of Israel out of exile to return home (v. 7). Such compassion reverses the "hiding of God's face" by extending to Israel God's *hesed*, or everlasting love (v. 8). Such compassion serves as the guarantor of the promise of a new covenant of God's *shalom* that will not be removed. Compassion is God's final word to Israel.

The utter reversal in situation between abandonment and compassion is signified in Isaiah's appeal to the imagery of the Noah story. The flood was a catastrophic devastation, an abandonment that boggles faith's imagination. But when the waters subsided, and the flood's survivors disembarked, God resolved to do things differently. Nothing had changed in the human heart (Genesis 6:5; 9:21). The difference now came in God's promise of "never again"—and the rainbow that assured that promise. In Isaiah 54, a similar new beginning is promised. The abandonment by God, acknowledged without being explained, will give way to the compassion of God. God's *shalom* and compassionate love will endure. Do you believe that? Do you trust your self and your hope to that? Is that final word of God's compassion the basis of how you conduct your life and live toward the future? To do so is to make a leap of faith, a leap that begins in the opening of Isaiah's text: in the acknowledgment of abandonment, where God's face goes hidden from us in experiences that cause us grief and threaten us with despair.

Israel in exile was not the last time people wondered where God was when things went haywire. For some, that wondering leads to rejection of God. For some, that wondering leads to fanciful denials that nothing really went wrong since God *intended* some grotesque tragedy to occur. For others, such as Ann Weems, that wondering leads to deeper faith not by trying to make sense of what makes no sense but by not letting go of God, whether in lament or praise or silence. In the face of mystery, holy or otherwise, faith trusts God's final word to be *compassion*.

NOTE

1. Ann Weems, *Psalms of Lament* (Louisville: Westminster John Knox Press, 1995), preface.

Holy God, Compassionate God, I would trust you. I would trust you, even when I cannot see you. I would trust you, even when you seem far away. I would trust you and your love with the whole of my life, my joys, my aches, my fears, and my faith. For in the end, you are the One who endures, and your compassion is what makes that enduring my hope. In Jesus Christ. Amen.

chapter 6

LOVE AS
WONDER

This book has viewed "love" in the biblical works from a variety of perspectives. Gift. Invitation. Loyalty. Ethic. Compassion. And now, in this closing chapter, we come to love as wonder. Wonder is as inclusive a characteristic of love in the biblical witness as exists. When we receive and when we give love, love bears the possibility of transporting us and others out of the realm of the ordinary into the regions of wonder.

In our everyday language, *wonder* suggests the feeling of awe or astonishment. If we do not experience such wonder when we realize that the Power who spun the universe is the One who loves us and all of creation, we may not have fully grasped what is going on. The biblical witness often links the terms "signs and wonders." Wonders, and wonder, testify to the connection with and experience of the Holy in our midst. By the grace of God, the wonder generated in holy encounter comes to fruition most profoundly in knowing ourselves and others as those who are loved and called to love by God. That is our identity, that is our vocation, until the final stanza of the hymn *Love Divine, All Loves Excelling* comes to pass: "till we cast our crowns before thee, lost in wonder, love, and praise."

Holy Ground, Holy Love   Exodus 34:1-10

What do you hold as holy ground? Some folks may hold ancestral lands or places in such esteem. Years ago, on a visit to our former exchange student in Germany, our family set out on a genealogical side trip. We were armed with a copy of a note from a church in St. Louis that indicated the town and year of my great-grandfather's baptism. We had several fortunate breaks that day, and by late afternoon our AFS student and his mother were translating the words of a man whose mother was my great-grandfather's younger sister. The house in which we visited with him had been built around 1900, he said, the third such residence on that lot since the seventeenth century. According to family folklore, those homes had been continuously lived in by Indermarks all through that time. If not holy in the literal sense of the term, that place was surely special ground for me. It was home ground, where journeys had started.

What makes a place special, or holy, are the connections and the stories it "stores." In the sacred geography of Judaism, few places rival Mount Sinai (sometimes called Horeb) for holiness of ground. According to Exodus 19 and 20, Mount Sinai is the holy mountain where Moses received the stone tablets upon which the Ten Commandments were written. But that familiar story is not the one related to Sinai in Exodus 34. Among the narratives in the intervening thirteen chapters, none are more critical than the stories of Chapters 32–33. The people built and worshiped a golden calf in Moses' absence. Even after a rather horrific "cleansing" that left three thousand dead, more bad news follows. God tells Moses to take the people to the Promised Land—only now, there is a new stipulation. "But I will not go up among you, or I would consume you on the way, for you are a stiff-necked people" (33:3). In other words, God will part company from Israel. It is an astounding declaration. Whatever holy ground there has been in the past because of God's holy presence, it will now be just that: in the past. God has had enough.

Sinai becomes holy once again, though, thanks to the intervention of Moses. The God who signed off on Israel signs back on in response to the intercession of Moses (33:12-17). Stories of holy ground made sacred by God's presence will not be relegated to distant times and bygone sojourners. God will continue to companion the people. The guarantor of that promise of holy presence comes in a remarkable self-disclosure of God's holy love: "The LORD, the LORD, / a God merciful and gracious, / slow to anger, / and abounding in steadfast love and faithfulness, / keeping steadfast love for the thousandth generation" (34:6-7a). Sinai first became holy ground because of the law God delivered there. Sinai now becomes holy ground because of the love God assured there.

So tell me, friend, where is your Sinai? Where is the place, the experience, in which you have been awestruck in wonder at the depth and breadth of God's love for you, for the world, for the ones you love, and for the ones you could just as well do without? Where is the holy ground that reveals to you that God is ultimately not the One whose power threatens to undo you unless you toe the line, but the One whose power seeks to love you back into life and trust.

Such places, such experiences, can become turning points when we recognize them as holy. The reason for that? When we draw face-to-face with the truth that God's essential character is that of keeping steadfast love for more generations than we can imagine, we may cease to be scared of God and freed to trust God's gracious love. We may cease our efforts at placating God in the realization that God's mercy empowers us to serve God for the sheer joy of it. When we can find such ground to plant our trust upon, when we can offer such ground for others who seek peace and purpose, we stand on holy ground.

It is ground made holy and wondrous by the gracious assurance that God's nature and promise is to give us steadfast love. It is ground made holy and wondrous by the stories that call us back to that love when we find ourselves assaulted or seduced by other words that beckon us to fear or hate others, ourselves, or God. What do you hold as sacred ground? What are the experiences and stories that convince you that you stand on holy ground as you stand in the wondrous grace of God's love?

Create an art image, or a journal entry, that reflects on the places—and the ones—you associate with what is "holy ground" for you. Reflect in that creation your sense of wonder at what holy ground—and holy love—brings to you.

When Wonder Is Not Delight   Mark 10:17-22

"If you really loved me, you would_____." How would you fill in that blank based on the last time someone spoke those words to you—or based on the last time you spoke those words to someone? The operative assumption in such a request is that love should do what is being asked. No doubt, there are many times those words are coupled with a request that is not only fair but absolutely necessary. *If you loved me, you'd stop hitting me. If you loved me, you'd include me in the decision-making. If you loved me, you'd . . .*

On the other hand, there are times when those words are coupled with a request that is entirely self-serving or other-demeaning. Think of the request made by the prodigal in Luke's parable. It is as if he asks his father at the outset, "If you loved me, you'd give me my inheritance." Think of a time when someone tried to manipulate you or when you tried to manipulate another with such an appeal. For teenagers experimenting in the delicate dance of relationship and intimacy, the phrase can serve as leverage to secure the next step on the physical intimacy scale. The same is true for adults who manipulate partners to excuse some behavior: "If you loved me, you'd call the boss and tell him I'm sick and not hungover." For some, love gets twisted into a form of control to get what we want, because if we love someone, that means we will give that person whatever she or he wants. Right?

Please underscore the word *want* in that last sentence. "Want" is where *if you loved me, you'd* . . . gets the best of us in trouble. Far closer to the gospel truth would be to substitute "need" for "want." To love another does seek to meet the loved one's deepest need, his or her ultimate good.

But the substitution of "need" for "want" in what we seek of love for ourselves, and others, creates tension. To love another, or to be loved by another, in a way that addresses needs rather than wants can be misunderstood. It is why love's wonder may not always bring delight.

Consider the story from Mark's Gospel referenced at the top of this reading. A well-to-do young man comes to Jesus on a spiritual journey. He is not new to this journey, for he clearly has kept his tradition's path for godly and godward living. But something apparently is still missing. Something moves this quite commendable individual to ask Jesus what way he should take. Imagine someone like this coming to your congregation: a young adult, a genuine seeker of things spiritual. I suspect more than one of us would pat him on the back, sign him in the guest register, and ask if he'd ever considered teaching Sunday school or serving on the board.

The critical element in this story comes as Mark describes how Jesus viewed this young man: "Jesus, looking at him, loved him." Whoa! You just know things are going to go well now. Jesus *loves* this guy. So what does Jesus bestow on this upright, outstanding, we-need-more-young-people-like-this-in-our-pews candidate for discipleship whom Jesus looks at and loves? *Go and sell what you have, give it all to the poor; and then, come and follow me.*

That's love?

Apparently, that's pretty much the response of this young seeker to Jesus. His reaction is shock and grief. He walks away, I would daresay, *wondering*.

Perhaps we are tempted to walk away wondering ourselves. Really now, all this young man wanted was a clue about eternal life. But Jesus' love was not content to offer this seeker what he *wanted*. Jesus moved the encounter from *want* to *need*—"you lack one thing" (to lack is to be in need).

Would the young man have been happier if Jesus' love had given him what he wanted? I suspect so, at least in the short term. But is the primary aim of love—at least such love as God brings to us and seeks from us—to make others (or ourselves) happier, or to make others (or ourselves) better? In the long run, to be made better should make one happier. But in the moment when love seeks what is best for another, what is needed by another, rather than the other's momentary wish list, there is the possibility that love will not be interpreted as loving. The choice of such love is inevitable in parenting. The choice of such love is inevitable in the church. As important as comfort can be, to love one another is not always and everywhere to make each other always feel good or do just what is wanted.

When such love is exercised, it may leave others and it may leave us wondering. And that is all right. For wonder, whether joyful or awe-stricken, moves us to look deeper. In doing so, wonder may actually make it possible for those who walk away, shocked and grieved, to realize down the road that love sought their good and not just their pleasure—and seeks it still.

Think back on a time and experience when you did not recognize an act of love extended your way, and perhaps even rejected it. What was it that stood between you and the recognition of love at that time? What has enabled you to come to see that as an act of love? How has that whole experience shaped you and shaped your faith?

Of All the Places   Jeremiah 31:1-3

Before my final year at seminary, I served a year-long internship at Second U.C.C. in Portland. It was a church that initially served Swiss Reformed folks in the early 1900s. It enjoyed modest growth until its heyday in the late 1940s and 1950s. Then, a new sanctuary was built, the Sunday school boomed, and all was well. But like many other mainline congregations in the 1960s, things went south. Membership and worship attendance declined. Once-bustling Sunday school rooms had little activity. It was a wilderness time in the life of the congregation. In the 1970s the congregation was served by an energetic and visionary retired interim pastor, who convinced one generous member to fund an intern program. The hope was that having a young person in ministry might attract new, young families. Two of us came as interns, and I can't say that we fulfilled those hopes.

In the midst of that wilderness time at Second Church, they began a sojourn with a small African American U.C.C. congregation named St. Andrews. It too was in a wilderness situation: small numbers, aging facility, served by another retired but energetic and visionary pastor and a youthful assistant. During my year at Second Church, we shared a church picnic with St. Andrews, did at least one pulpit exchange, and I made several pastoral calls on St. Andrews members when their clergy were unavailable. Nothing earthshaking. But tentative steps were being made together by these two communities. The steps continued and eventually paved the way, almost a decade later, for two deaths and a birth. The two deaths were Second and St. Andrews, and the simultaneous birth was of Ainsworth United Church of Christ. It was not a merger but a new creation that graciously came out of those wilderness times.

"The people who survived . . . / found grace in the wilderness" (31:2). Jeremiah wrote these words to a community beleaguered by life in the wilderness of Babylon's exile. There was no going back to what had been, no magic wand to wave and turn the clock back. Jeremiah's promise—and it was still a promise, not a fulfillment—was that the wilderness would become the place of grace. Jeremiah's assurance that the transformation of wilderness from a struggle to survive to an experience of new life came in the form of God's love and faithfulness.

Jeremiah's words and promise bring to my mind what happened with Second and St. Andrews churches. Easier paths were possible. For Second Church, it would have been tempting to live in the illusion of nostalgia, to deny the change that had come and the wilderness through which they journeyed. That path would have kept them doing the same things done in years past during the church's golden era when those things worked. But they hadn't worked for a while. Sometimes we do keep doing things over and over again because that's all we know or that's all we dare. Keep in mind the perspective often attributed to Albert Einstein: "The definition of insanity is doing the same thing over and over again and expecting different results." Wilderness offers the potentially liberating challenge of shedding what no longer works and risking the new. Another, easier way for those congregations would have been to curl up and die. It would have been easy to take the signs of decline as irreversible and adopt the attitude of enjoying each other's company until the last one standing remembers to turn out the light on the way out. I suspect there are times and situations when that is the best choice possible, at least in terms of helping congregations come to grips with the seriousness of what stands before them. Jeremiah points us to wilderness as a transformative place. Wilderness can become that turning point where we shed the illusions cast by false hope and false despair and choose to rely on the grace and love of God for the way ahead.

For Second Church and St. Andrews, wilderness times brought recognition of a new experience of God's grace and a new way to be the church. The "dying" of the two for the sake of the "rising" of Ainsworth reveals a willingness to take such promises as Jeremiah's to heart. For me, it is a wondrous thing to see what has happened. The goal of new and young families for which interns were once hired has now become the very real and lived truth of this blended congregation. The grace they have received of God has become the graciousness with which they embrace folks across lines of race and sexual orientation and economic status that, I suspect, neither of their predecessors may have dared alone.

Grace in the wilderness is a promise and hope to which God calls both congregations and individuals. In our wilderness times God offers us the opportunity to shed the baggage we no longer need and the fears that hold us back, all for the sake of discovering who we are and whose we are. Like the people of Israel, we are people blessed with God's everlasting and faithful love.

Is there a place of "wilderness" in your life? In your spiritual journey? Is there a place and a time where you search between a past that you have let go or that has been taken from you and a future that is still not clear? Read aloud Jeremiah 31:2-3, substituting your name for "the people." What grace might God be offering to you in this wilderness time? How might you open yourself to the wonder and surprise of such grace to be found in this wilderness?

Out of Sight   1 Peter 1:8-9

My one and only experience of flying on a small commuter aircraft came on a round-trip excursion from Astoria, Oregon, to Portland. The flight from Astoria was terrific. The day was absolutely clear. I was the only passenger. To keep the plane's weight balanced, the pilot had me sit in what would have been the copilot's seat had there been a copilot. Besides being very careful not to step on the floor controls beneath me, I thoroughly enjoyed watching us cruise over the Columbia and then the northern hills of the Coastal Range before landing. The return trip, several days later, was entirely different. There were a few more passengers, maybe five. Shortly after takeoff, we ascended into the clouds. For the rest of the flight, I looked out the front window and saw exactly what the pilot saw—nothing. I have flown on large commercial airliners many times and was never concerned when the view out the side windows was obliterated by clouds. But now, in this small, prop-driven craft, looking out the front window and seeing nothing but a whiteout was disconcerting. I don't know what I was thinking. Perhaps it was supposed to be clearer up there so the pilot could "drive" more safely. What that flight brought home to me was the trust inherent in instrument flying. When the way forward is literally out of sight, you have to trust that the instruments will take you home.

The analogy is far from perfect, but journeying by faith requires such trust. First Peter addresses a community that is second- and perhaps even third-generation Christian. These are followers who never set eyes on Jesus, who never heard firsthand the stories or saw as eyewitnesses the miracles and healings. That was the lingering reality of Jesus' ascension. Jesus no longer walked among the disciples as he once did. No longer was there the luxury of sharing the immediate presence of Jesus, of attending to his words, or asking questions when those words are misunderstood. With the Ascension, Jesus had left the building, so to speak.

Like this community, we live in the wake of the Ascension. We live as those for whom faith's journey and relationship with Christ relies far more on trust of the heart than sight of the eyes. John's Gospel prepared the disciples for this in the narrative of Thomas, who would not believe unless he saw Jesus' wounds. Jesus appeared, showed his wounds to Thomas, and said to him, "Blessed are those who have not seen and yet have come to believe" (John 20:24-29). It is not just belief at stake here, 1 Peter 1:8 clearly points out: "Although you have not *seen* him, you *love* him" (italics added). The Christian journey is not simply a matter of belief, or even trust. The Christian journey is first and foremost a matter of love. On this journey, even the inability to see Jesus does not get in the way of this community's ability and calling to love Christ and to love all those whom Christ loves.

Recall an experience where you found yourself having, in faith, to "fly by instrument," that is, to trust that there would be a way forward even when nothing was clear at that moment. In what ways did that experience shape your faith? In what ways might that experience shape the way you exercise love for others, including the ones for whom you see no apparent reason to love?

CAN'T BUY ME LOVE   SONG of SOLOMON 8:6-7

With all due respect to John Lennon and Paul McCartney for their version of "Can't Buy Me Love," they were not the first to lyricize that truth. Song of Solomon 8:7 nailed the theme three millennia earlier: "If one offered for love / all the wealth of one's house, / it would be utterly scorned." In a world where it seems that everything—and some argue, every*one*—has a price, love defies the gravitational force of the marketplace and soars free. Such freedom is subversive, at least from the point of view of those who have the resources to presume they can and thus should be able to have anything or anyone they choose. In strictly human terms, this subversive nature of love fuels the stories of loves that cut against the grain of arranged marriages and class relationships. In spiritual terms, it recalls the story of Simon Magus in Acts 8, a magician of considerable fame who was baptized as the result of Philip's preaching. Later, when Peter and John came to Samaria, they laid their hands on the converts, who then received the Holy Spirit. Simon Magus approached the two apostles and offered to pay them for such power to bestow God's Spirit. Their rebuke of his proposition made it clear that Spirit, like love, cannot be purchased.

If love shares with Spirit the inability to be secured by money, the wonder of love is that it, like Spirit, possesses extraordinary power. That wondrous nature of love also finds poetic expression in Song of Solomon: "love is strong as death . . . / Many waters cannot quench love" (vv. 6, 7). What, in your experience, have you found stronger than death? Do not think of this in terms of a philosophical reflection on an abstract idea. Think of this in terms of a time when you stood at the graveside of a friend or loved one. In that place and time, what seemed stronger to you than the reality of the casket being lowered, or the urn with ashes being interred? What was it that allowed you to walk away from that experience with anything more than despair at such finality? Love brings to such experiences the possibility of strength, the potential for hope, and the promise of life. It may come through love shared with the one now departed. It may come through love imparted by the community that surrounds you and goes with you from that place. And it certainly may be the love in which God holds you, and holds that one from whom you are now separated. Paul bore testimony to such love in Romans 8, where nothing "in all creation, will be able to separate us from the love of God in Christ Jesus our Lord" (8:39). Do you trust such love to be stronger than death?

Song of Solomon brings another affirmation of love's power arising out of an earlier image of love as fire: "many waters cannot quench love, / neither can floods drown it" (v. 7). I remember the campfire training from Scouting days and Forest Service signs: spread out the coals, pour water, stir the water into the coals, and repeat the routine until the fire is out. Don't trust a fire is extinguished because there are no flames. Fires can burn deep, even underground.

So imagine a fire that cannot be quenched, no matter how much water or retardant is applied. Love bears such potential in our lives. Love can endure the most difficult and trying of times. Spouses and partners who have shared love for many years, families whose love has survived through economic turmoil and relational crises, friends whose love for one another has held even after years of separation or frank words are examples of love that will not be quenched or dampened by adversity.

Imagine, then, the love of God for you and for this world that likewise will not be quenched. We are held in a love that will not give up on us, that sees us as "my children" and "my creation." Our love for God invites similar tenacity to hold on to God in spite of what comes, to trust that God's love remains there in those times and experiences where it seems far removed, and to act on the basis of such love not only for us but for all. Many waters cannot quench such love, for in baptism's waters we are claimed by God's love.

No wonder such love cannot be bought. Love, as life itself, comes to us as a freely and graciously given gift. In Jesus Christ, God bestows the gift of love upon us (John 3:16). From Jesus Christ, we receive the call to gift God and one another with our love (Matthew 22:36-38). Gifts are for giving and receiving. So it is with love. Thanks be to God.

When have you experienced the irrepressible power of love? When have you experienced unconditional acceptance from another? When has such love made all the difference in a direction your life was taking? In your tenacity in loving another? Offer a prayer of thanks for the grace of love that has buoyed you up and for the privilege of offering such grace of love to another.

"THE GREATEST OF THESE"   1 CORINTHIANS 13

If a study could be made of the times when 1 Corinthians 13 has been read in public, we might be led to believe Paul wrote the chapter primarily for marriage ceremonies. Certainly the chapter bears much wisdom for those nervously perched at the threshold of beginning a new relationship as husband and wife. Paul, however, did not write these words to provide ministers and justices of the peace with something of substance for such moments. Paul wrote these words to the church at Corinth and, through them, to churches everywhere and in every time.

The message is simple: love is the keystone for Christian living. Putting love at center stage amounts to getting first things first. Without love, nothing else matters. The simplicity of the message, however, becomes enormously complicated as one seeks to translate the *word* of love into the *life* of love. Enabling such a translation from word to deed is what drives and enlivens Paul's relating of love's necessity, love's identity, and love's permanence in life.

The necessity of having such love finds illustration in the opening verses of the chapter. Paul makes reference there to highly prized qualities and actions that were experienced in Christian community. Ecstatic speech. Prophetic witness. Wisdom. Extraordinary acts of sacrifice. Yet, in each case, he writes that without the motive and expression of love, such acts come to nothing. Without love, the most eloquent of speech is just so much noise. Without love, prophecy and knowledge and even faith itself stand as empty posturing. Without love, the most generous of gifts, even the gift of self, gains nothing. Why? Love enlivens the language, inspires the knowledge, and kindles the offering.

Paul moves on to verses that identify such love in action. *Action* is the key word, for in all these verses Paul does not use a single adjective to describe love. All the descriptive words are verbs. Even though that truth does not carry over into our English translations, the point is important: love *is* only as love *does*. The church advances the cause of love not a single inch by wrapping it in rhetorical flourishes or doctrinal certainties. Love requires enactment and embodiment. Such love does not come easily or without struggle. Such love is not within our power alone. For its possibility, God gives us the example of Christ's own life and ministry. God gives us the freedom that comes from knowing that we are accepted and loved through God's grace. God gives us the presence of the Spirit to empower us to love as we have been loved.

Paul closes the chapter with a sort of "when all is said and done" conclusion that moves in the direction of love's permanence. He becomes somewhat philosophical in describing how the other gifts of prophecy and tongues and knowledge will all eventually pass away when that which is perfect has come. In a wonderfully rich image, he writes of this passing away as when a child matures and gives up those things that belong to childhood.

Paul, however, by no means claims that the time of perfection has come. We still live on the "not-yet" side of the full realization of God's kingdom. Now we see in a mirror dimly, now we know in part. Paul perceives in God's promises and love a time when our sight will not be as distortions reflected in a clouded mirror, as it is now. One day, we will see face to face. Our understanding will be complete—even as we are now understood completely by the One who bids our love.

In the summit of this text, Paul brings the words and images of love to their final statement: "And now *faith, hope, and love abide, these three; and the greatest of these is love*" (13:13, italics added). Faith will be replaced by our direct experience of that which we have for so long trusted. Hope will dissipate in fulfillment. Love will remain, however, and never be superseded, because God is love. Life lived in the presence of God will be life lived in love for all eternity.

Until then, love remains faith's greatest calling. Our other attainments only have value because love enlivens them. Without love, the grandest of speech is mute; but with love, the poorest words become gospel. Without love, the deepest understanding is akin to ignorance; but with love, the simplest thought becomes wisdom. Without love, the most sacrificial gift is empty of value; but with love, the widow's mite becomes extravagant. Faith, hope, and love abide; but the greatest of these is love.

"The greatest of these is love." Come prayerfully into the presence of God with these words, and linger there. Linger in love's gifts that surround you. Prayerfully consider those whom you love and those who love you. Consider God, whose love formed you and whose love you are graced to share with others. Be still, in the presence of God, in the joy and wonder of such love. When you leave this moment of meditation upon love, leave with love's gift to companion you this day and through all your days.

INTRODUCTION TO THE
LEADER'S GUIDE

The following two pages form a template that can be copied for use in planning each of the six suggested sessions. Space is provided on the template so that the copies made will have room for you to make notes on the activities and exercises you will use in each session.

The pages following the template contain a discussion guide for each chapter using questions based on their Scripture passages and accompanying devotional readings, along with a suggested group activity, as you plan each session. Use the space after the questions in the discussion guide for insights or ideas you would like to present to the group. Please distribute the books a minimum of one week ahead of the first session, with clear instructions to do the daily readings (one a day) prior to the first session. "Using This Book" (located in the introduction) provides guidance for doing the reading and exercises over the course of each week.

Feel free to adapt the suggested session focus of each chapter to meet the needs and interests of your group. You are encouraged to blend and incorporate the activities and exercises suggested here with your own ideas for engaging the group with each chapter.

SESSION TEMPLATE

SESSION FOCUS

[Summarizing the session's theme and intentions in a single sentence]

PREPARATION

[Gathering and arranging ahead of time what you will need for this session]

Meeting Space and Worship Center

Materials Needed

GATHERING

[Creating a welcoming and worshipful setting to introduce the focus]

Welcome and Introductions

Ritual

[See instructions in "For Every Session"]

Entering the Theme

REFLECTING

[Exploring this chapter's readings and their biblical moorings]

Biblical Background

Chapter Review

RESPONDING

[Engaging the insights into love generated by the readings and session]

Inward

Outward

BLESSING AND COMMISSIONING

[Being blessed and sent to love as God's people]

Review

Sending

FOR EVERY SESSION

- Create a visual focal point (worship center, display area) where images and symbols related to each session's theme can be exhibited from week to week.
- Six candles and lighter for the ritual used in "Gathering." Light one candle at the first session, two at the second, and so on.
- Bibles and extra copies of *The Greatest of These* for use by visitors, or in case participants leave theirs at home.
- If you plan to offer coffee or other refreshments, please have all the supplies on hand and prepared so that you or others do not expend session time on "chores."
- Newsprint sheets and markers; paper and pens.

DISCUSSION GUIDES

SESSION ONE "Love as Gift"
Scriptures: John 3:16-17; Isaiah 43:1-7; Deuteronomy 7:7-9; Romans 8:28; 1 John 4:16; Psalm 31:14-16

Focus: *God's gift of love grounds our faith and companions our discipleship in grace.*

Discussion and Reflection Questions

John. 3:16-17   What are the implications of "for God so loved the world": for your personal sense of being loved; for the way you view and respond to others and the world?

Isa. 43:1-7   Who have been "companions" on your faith journey? In what ways did their presence convey love's gift to you? How might you companion others?

Deut . 7:7-9   In what situations have you experienced wonder at the graciousness of God's choices? How might love's gift shape your own choices?

Rom. 8:28 What witness do you bring of "all things working together for good?" Where in those workings has the gift of God's love been embodied for you? How?

1 John 4:16 What deep memories, and/or recent experiences, convince you that God's gift to you is love?

Ps. 31:14-16 What experiences of love's gift lead you to entrust yourself into God's hands? What do you need to entrust into God's hands in this particular moment?

Group Activity Suggestion
Bring six gift-wrapped boxes. Place a slip of paper in each that records one of the six titles and Scripture references from the chapter's readings. Open boxes one at a time. Read the title and text reference inside. Discuss any questions or comments related to that reading in the book and/or Scripture passage. Encourage members to connect those readings and their own life experiences.

Closing
Lead the litany prayer at the end of the last section, "My Times Are in Your Hand."

SESSION TWO "Love As Invitation"
Scriptures: Song of Solomon 2:8-13; Hebrews 10:23-25; Amos 5:14-15; Jude 20-22; Deuteronomy 10:12-13; John 20:15-19

Focus: *God's love invites us to receive and practice its grace.*

Discussion and Reflection Questions

Song 2:8-13 Where at this moment in your faith journey do you experience the invitation to move away from isolation for the sake of expressing love?

Heb. 10:23-25 In what areas of faith might you, or your congregation, need a "provoking" to love? Where, and to whom, might you turn for such encouragement?

Amos 5:14-15 What practical implications, in your relationships and in your community, does the invitation to "love good" have? What can be the costs of such love?

Jude 20-22 What led you to fall in love with God? What now keeps you in that love?

Dt. 10:12-13 How do you understand seeking one's own good related to seeking the "common good?" What actions might love engage in that bind both of those yearnings?

Jn. 20:15-19 In what ways is love told and is love shown in your witness? In the mission of your church? How would others recognize love in those tellings and showings?

Group Activity Suggestion
Bring blank invitation cards for every participant. Distribute them after discussing the readings. Have them write their own names as the invitee. Where it calls for day and time, write "this week." In the space for the occasion, explain they will write two specific things they will do this week in response to God's love. One: *how will you be more receptive to the love God invites you to receive*? The other: *what new or renewed action will you take to put God's love into practice*?

Closing
Offer together as a commissioning the prayer that closes "For the Good of . . ."

SESSION THREE "Love as Loyalty"
Scriptures: Psalm 136; Deuteronomy 6:4-5; John 15:12-15; Colossians 3:14; Hosea 11:1-9; 1 Thessalonians 4:9-10

Focus: *God's persistent loyalty in love evokes our gratitude and empowers our love's loyalty.*

Discussion and Reflection Questions

Psalm 136   What comprises the "inventory" of your experiences of God's steadfast and loyal love? In what ways does remembering your experiences shape your practice of love?

Deut. 6:4-5   Where do you find the call to love God "with all" meeting resistance in your life? How might these places of challenge become places of growth for your faith?

Jn. 15:12-15   How is the dynamic of friendship reflected in the nature of Christian community? In what ways have you received, and extended, loyalty in these friendships?

Col. 3:14   What are the ties that bind you in and to Christian community? What movements do these bindings make possible in your life?

Hosea 11:1-9   How have experiences of disloyalty in love affected your ease at receiving or extending love? How do you understand Hosea's words in light of those experiences?

1 Th. 4:9-10   Whose loyalty to and interest in you spurred you on to achieve more than you might have otherwise? How do you express loyalty and interest in your love for God and others?

Group Activity Suggestion

Form teams of three or more. Assign each team one of the Scripture readings. Have the group create a skit that illustrates in a contemporary situation what their reading reveals about love and loyalty. Allow adequate time for planning. Have each team perform their skit. Discuss afterwards what insights into love as loyalty emerged.

Closing: Lead a litany of thanks to God. Have the participants offer a phrase or sentence expressing gratitude. After each phrase or sentence, the entire group will respond with the refrain: "For God's loyal love endures."

SESSION FOUR   "Love as Ethic"
Scriptures: Romans 13:1-8; Isaiah 61:1-3, 8; John 13:35; Leviticus 19:13-18; 1 John 4:20-21; Psalm 85:7-13

Focus: *God's love, and the justice God loves, provides the basis and compass for our ethics.*

Discussion and Reflection Questions

Rom. 13:1-8   To whom are your debts of love most clearly owed, and for what? Where do you see the challenges in your life, in the culture around you, and in your congregation to owe no one anything but love?

Isa. 61:1-3, 8   How might "I the LORD love justice" transform our usual motives or appeals to do justice? What perspective might it lend to how we view those in need of justice?

John 13:35   "See, how they love one another." What might convince a visitor that those words describe your congregation? Or, what verbs might they be led to substitute for "love"?

Lev. 19:13-18 How does our understanding of "neighbor" translate into limits or possibilities for heeding love's command? What limits are a lively issue in your community?

1 Jn. 4:20-21 Where in your faith journey do you most struggle with matters of integrity? Where do you see the church struggling with integrity in the realm of love?

Ps. 85:7-13 Where today do you perceive, even if in limited ways, the kiss of righteousness and peace? In what ways might we work with God to advance that union?

Group Activity Suggestion

Adapt the exercise at the end of "Loving What God Loves" for use by the group. Do the responsive reading, with individuals reading the "action" lines and the group offering the designated refrain. Identify a justice issue for which the group has passion. Decide a specific action to be taken, individually and/or together, in response to God's love for justice.

Closing: Commission the group to action with Isaiah 61:1-2, substituting "you" for "me."

SESSION FIVE "Love as Compassion"

Scriptures: Deuteronomy 10:17-19; Hebrews 13:1-2; 1 Samuel 18:1-4, 20:12-17; Philippians 2:1-5; Matthew 5:43-48; Isaiah 54:7-10

Focus: *God's compassionate love beckons us to Christ-centered empathy that risks self for others.*

Discussion and Reflection Questions

Dt. 10:17-19 Who have been your mentors in the practice of Christian compassion and love? What have you learned by experience of God's compassionate love?

Heb. 13:1-2 What practices of hospitality and compassion do you and/or your congregation engage in that embody Hebrews' welcoming of strangers and outsiders?

1 Sm. 18:1-4, "To love another as self." Where have you
20:12-17 seen or experienced such compassion? Where might such love need to be risked? By you? By your congregation?

Phil. 2:1-5 Where do you witness the connection between having the mind of Christ and practicing the compassion of Christ? In what ways do you live that connection?

Matt. 5:43-48 When Jesus says, "love your enemies," what do you say and do in return? What do you find most extreme about the call to love with compassion?

Isa. 54:7-10 Have you ever known a "brief moment" of feeling abandoned by God? What led you to that moment? What led you out of it? Where do you locate compassion in that experience?

Group Activity Suggestion

Bring materials for creating a collage (or more than one, if your group is large): posterboard, pictorial magazines, newspapers, markers, scissors, tape. Have participants create a collage on the theme of love as compassion. For added direction, encourage them to use one or more images, headlines, or drawings that illustrate each of the titles of this chapter's readings.

Closing

Offer in unison the prayer that closes "To Love Another as Self."

SESSION SIX "Love as Wonder"
Scriptures: Exodus 34:1-10; Mark 10:17-22; Jeremiah 31:1-3;
1 Peter 1:8-9; Song of Solomon 8:6-7; 1 Corinthians 13

Focus: *God's love provokes awe-filled wonder at the truth that the*
Holy God embraces you and me and all.

Discussion and Reflection Questions

Ex. 34:1-10   What is holy ground for you? What are the places and relationships where you have encountered God? How is such ground a source of wonder at God's love?

Mk. 10:17-22 When did your love for another, or another's love for you, ask a hard thing that left you or that other wondering? What aspects of God's love for you or for others leave you wondering?

Jer. 31:1-3   What "wilderness" confronts your faith journey? Your congregation's journey? In what ways might the grace of God's love be found in that wilderness?

1 Pet. 1:8-9 When have you found yourself trusting while not seeing your way forward in some trying situation? In what ways did love propel or beckon you in your way ahead?

Song 8:6-7   When have you wondered at the power and endurance of love in the midst of joy or in the face of grief? What have you learned in that wondering?

1 Cor. 13   In what ways have you experienced love's greatness in its gift to you? In its challenge for you?

Group Activity Suggestion
Adapt the exercise at the end of "The Greatest of These" into a
guided meditation. Invite participants to close their eyes, take several

deep breaths, and be in a spirit of openness and wonder. Proceed by reading the exercise, pausing after phrases or sentences to allow time for reflection. Close by inviting participants to open their eyes. Invite them to share thoughts or feelings inspired by the prayerful meditation.

Closing
Sing "Will You Come and Follow Me?" or "Love Divine, All Loves Excelling."